ESCHATOLOGY
AND THE
NEW TESTAMENT

ESCHATOLOGY

AND THE

NEW TESTAMENT

Essays in Honor of
George Raymond Beasley-Murray

EDITED BY W. HULITT GLOER

 HENDRICKSON
PUBLISHERS
PEABODY, MASSACHUSETTS 01961-3473

Copyright © 1988.
Hendrickson Publishers, Inc.
P.O. Box 3473
Peabody, Massachusetts 01961–3473
All rights reserved.
Printed in the United States of America

ISBN 0–943575–01–X

TABLE OF CONTENTS

EDITOR'S PREFACE

The essays in this volume are presented in honor of Professor George Raymond Beasley-Murray by long-time friends and colleagues. The names of the contributors read like a "Who's Who" of twentieth-century New Testament studies. This is, of course, as it should be in any tribute to one whose name certainly belongs in such esteemed company. Indeed, few people have contributed more to the advancement of biblical scholarship and to the ongoing life of the church than the honoree of this volume.

Born in London on October 10, 1916, Professor Beasley-Murray received his early education at the City of Leicester Boys' School and seemed headed for a career in music. He writes, "At the romantic age of 16 the appeal of music was at its highest and I spent so many hours on the piano my mind was never free from music in any waking moment. I walked, cycled, worked, ate, and drank to its accompaniment (often in time to it!) and it invaded my sleep."[1] It was about this time, however, that he responded to the call to faith in Christ. He describes the impact of this decision in these words:

> The thrill of my entry in to life in Christ bit deep into me. The wonder of God's love for people like me, the marvel of Christ's victory over sin and death in His resurrection, the breathtaking hope of his coming in glory to share the power of His resurrection with all men, all this made a deep impression upon me. When I grasped these things and saw their implications for me I felt that everybody ought to know them. More explicitly, it seemed to me that since God had made them known to *me*, I ought also to make them known to others. I believed, therefore, that God had called me to know Christ and to make Christ known. He had brought me to himself that I might be a preacher.[2]

This commitment "to know Christ and to make Christ known" would become the motivating factor for his every decision from that time forward. He enrolled in London's Spurgeon's College to begin his preparation for ministry. While he was still

---

1. "My Call to the Ministry," in *My Call to the Ministry,* ed. C. A. Joyce (London: Marshall, Morgan and Scott, 1968) 37–38.
2. Ibid., 37.

a student there, World War II broke out; his experiences in wartime London would serve to strengthen his commitment "to make Christ known." Personal reflections on this dark period in his nation's history are telling:

> . . . We remained in London throughout the war. When the bombing began and we on our high point in South London at night watched bombs exploding and houses disintegrating, it was not easy to perceive the relevance of some of the controversies of early Church history and the like which we were studying. Yet we realized that what was taking place before our eyes was precisely the result of the denial of the Faith for which we stood, and its replacement by godless philosophies and creeds, whose effect was destruction and misery. When I was asked by an acquaintance in those days, "How do you feel now about the ministry and Christianity?" I replied that I had never been so convinced of the need of the Christian Faith and of ministers to proclaim it to the world. The passing of the years has deepened that conviction. Never has the world been so desperately in need of the Gospel of Christ and of men to make it known as it is now.[3]

Such is the nature of the conviction that has motivated Professor Beasley-Murray throughout the years of his ministry, a ministry that has included both the church and the classroom. Upon receiving the B.D. from Spurgeon's College, he continued his education at King's College, University of London, where he received the M.Th. (1948), Ph.D. (1952), and D.D. (1968) and at Jesus College, Cambridge from which he received the M.A. in 1950. He has also been awarded the D.D. (Hon.) from the McMaster Divinity College in Hamilton, Ontario, Canada. From 1941 to 1948 he served as the pastor of the Baptist church in Ilford, Essex and from 1948 to 1950 he served as Pastor of the Zion Baptist Church in Cambridge.

In 1950 he was called from the pastoral ministry to the specialized task of preparing others for the ministry. He began this ministry as Lecturer in New Testament at Spurgeon's College from 1950 to 1956. From 1956 to 1958 he served as professor of New Testament at the Baptist Theological Seminary in Ruschlikon, Switzerland. Then in 1958 he was called back to London to assume the post of principal of Spurgeon's College, a position he held until 1973. In that year, he was appointed the James Buchanan Harrison Professor of New Testament Interpretation at The Southern Baptist Theological Seminary in Louis-

3. Ibid., 39.

ville, Kentucky where he holds the position of Senior Professor of New Testament. In 1980 he returned to his beloved England where he continues to pursue a vigorous schedule of speaking and writing when not engaged in his teaching responsibilities.

These many years in the classroom have been marked by an enduring commitment to and involvement in the life of the church around the world. In 1962 he applied his musical expertise as a member of the committee responsible for compiling the Baptist Union hymnbook. From 1968 to 1969 he served as the president of the Baptist Union of Great Britain and Ireland, and in 1969 he served as the first chairman of the Baptist Union Council. He has been extremely active in the Baptist World Alliance for more than 30 years. Furthermore, he has actively participated in the Faith and Order Commission of the World Council of Churches. All along the way he has been in constant demand as a preacher and Bible teacher in local churches and local, national and international Bible conferences.

As a scholar Professor Beasley-Murray has demonstrated an expertise in many areas of study, a fact made clear by a quick glance at the bibliography of his writings. He has produced commentaries on Matthew, the General Epistles, 2 Corinthians, Philippians, and Ezekiel. His book, *Baptism in the New Testament,* published in 1962, has become a standard work on that subject and is already regarded as a classic. Beginning with the publication of *Jesus and the Future* in 1954, he has devoted significant attention to matters related to eschatology and the kingdom of God. In addition to having published numerous articles on that subject, he has also written a significant commentary on Book of Revelation. At the time of this writing, he had just completed a forthcoming critical commentary on the Fourth Gospel. The recent publication of his *Jesus and the Kingdom of God* shares the fruits of a lifetime of concentrated study in this area. It seems destined to become a standard work on this topic. It is altogether fitting, therefore, that the essays in this volume focus on the area of eschatology.

As a scholar, teacher, and preacher Professor Beasley-Murray has offered countless persons, including myself, a distinctive model of how careful biblical scholarship and the service of the church not only can but must go hand in hand. It was my privilege to serve as his Graduate Fellow for two years while a student at The Southern Baptist Theological Seminary and then to write my dissertation under his direction. My service as the editor of this volume is offered with deepest gratitude to him. It has been for me a "labor of love" in the truest sense. Hopefully it will make the kind of significant contribution to New Testament studies that its honoree continues to make.

I speak for all who have participated in the process of making this volume a reality when I offer this paraphrase of Paul's thanksgiving for the Philippians (1:4-5) as an ongoing salute to our dear colleague, teacher, and friend:

We thank God for every remembrance of you . . . thankful for your partnership in the gospel from the first day until now.

TABULA GRATULATORIA

Paul J. Achtemeier
Barbara Aland
Kurt Aland
David Balch
C. K. Barrett
S. Scott Bartchy
Markus Barth
Paul Beasley-Murray
Ernest Best
Hans Dieter Betz
J. Nelville Birdsall
Matthew Black
Gerald L. Borchert
John Wick Bowman
Raymond E. Brown
F. F. Bruce
Donald A. Carson
David Catchpole
J. H. Charlesworth
Ronald Clements
William B. Coble
David Coffey
Bruce Corley
John M. Court
C. E. B. Cranfield
Lorin L. Cranford
R. Alan Culpepper
Frederick William Danker
David Daube
Peter H. Davids
Karl Paul Donfried
John Drane
James D. G. Dunn

J. K. Elliott
E. Earle Ellis
C. F. Evans
Owen E. Evans
Gordon D. Fee
Fred L. Fisher
Joseph A. Fitzmyer
W. F. Flemington
J. Massyngbaerde Ford
Robert T. Fortna
Richard T. France
David E. Garland
Robert Garrett
Donald A. Hagner
Everett F. Harrison
Clayton K. Harrop
Gerald F. Hawthorne
Charles W. Hedrick
Martin Hengel
David Hill
T. R. Hobbs
Robert Hodgson, Jr.
Harold W. Hoehner
Morna D. Hooker
J. L. Houlden
Philip E. Hughes
William E. Hull
Richard L. Jeske
Robert Jewett
Sherman E. Johnson
Peter Rhea Jones
Leander E. Keck
Howard Clark Kee

Jack Dean Kingsbury
Robert A. Kraft
Edgar Krentz
Larry Krietzer
Werner G. Kümmel
Robert Kysar
Jan Lambrecht
William L. Lane
Thomas D. Lea
Andrew T. Lincoln
Barnabas Lindars
John F. Maile
John Marsh
I. Howard Marshall
Ralph Martin
Roger Martin
J. Louis Martyn
Edgar V. McKnight
Bruce M. Metzger
Robert P. Meye
Ben F. Meyer
J. Ramsey Michaels
Otto Michel
Paul S. Minear
Derek Moore-Crispin
Robert Morgan
W. G. Morrice
Leon Morris
Charles Francis Digby Moule
Michael K. Nicholls
D. E. Nineham
J. C. O'Neill
H. P. Owen
Robert F. O'Toole
Alan Pain
John Painter
Pierson Parker
Heber F. Peacock

David W. Perkins
Rudolf Pesch
John Polhill
John Reumann
John Riches
Mathias Rissi
Vernon K. Robbins
Walter Schmithals
Rudolf Schnackenburg
David M. Scholer
David Schroeder
Bernard Brandon Scott
Jeff Sharp
Stephen S. Smalley
D. Moody Smith
Richard A. Spencer
R. Wayne Stacy
Frank Stagg
Graham N. Stanton
James S. Stewart
Peter Stuhlmacher
G. M. Styler
J. P. M. Sweet
William R. Telford
Gerd Theissen
Anthony Thiselton
Stephen H. Travis
Allison A. Trites
Christopher M. Tuckett
Eduard Schwiezer
Günter Wagner
William O. Walker, Jr.
Hans Weder
David Wenham
John Wenham
R. McL. Wilson
Nigel G. Wright
Frances Young

A SELECT BIBLIOGRAPHY OF THE WRITINGS OF GEORGE RAYMOND BEASLEY-MURRAY

I. Books

Christ is Alive! London: Lutterworth, 1947.

Jesus and the Future: An Examination of the Eschatological Discourse, Mark 13, with Special Reference to the Little Apocalypse Theory. London: Macmillan, 1954.

Preaching the Gospel from the Gospels. Philadelphia: Judson, 1956.

A Commentary on Mark 13. London: Macmillan, 1957.

Baptism in the New Testament. London: Macmillan, 1962; Grand Rapids: Eerdmans, 1973.

The Resurrection of Jesus Christ. London: Oliphants, 1964.

The General Epistles: James, 1 Peter, Jude, 2 Peter. New York: Abingdon, 1965.

Baptism Today and Tomorrow. London: Macmillan, 1966; New York: St. Martin's, 1966.

The Gospel of John; a Commentary. Oxford: B. Blackwell, 1971.

Highlights in the Book of Revelation. Nashville: Broadman, 1972.

The Book of Revelation. New Century Bible. London: Oliphants, 1974.

Revelation: Three Viewpoints. Nashville: Broadman, 1977.

The Coming of God. Exeter: Paternoster Press, 1983.

Matthew. London: Scripture Press, 1984.

Jesus and the Kingdom of God. Grand Rapids: Eerdmans, 1986.

The Gospel of John. Word Biblical Commentary Series. Waco: Word, 1988.

II. Contributions to Books

"Ezekiel." *New Bible Commentary.* Wheaton, Ill.: Tyndale Press, 1953.

"Revelation." *New Bible Commentary.* Wheaton, Ill.: Tyndale Press, 1953.

"Baptism in the Letters of Paul." *Christian Baptism.* Edited by A. Gilmore. Philadelphia: Judson Press, 1959.

"Philippians." *Peake's Commentary on the Bible.* 2nd ed. Middlesex: Thomas Nelson & Sons Ltd., 1962.

"The Apostolic Writings." In *Roads Converge.* Edited by P.

Gardner-Smith. E. Arnold, 1963.

"Introduction to the New Testament." In *A Companion to the Bible,* 2nd ed. Edited by H. H. Rowley. Edinburgh: T. & T. Clark, 1963.

"Die Taufe der Glaubigen." In *Die Baptisten.* Edited by J. D. Hughey. Stuttgart: Evangelisches Verlagswerk, 1964.

"The Diaconate in Baptist Churches." In *The Ministry of Deacons.* World Council Studies 2. Geneva: World Council of Churches, 1965.

"My Call to the Ministry." In *My Call to the Ministry.* Edited by C. A. Joyce. London: Marshall, Morgan and Scott, Ltd., 1968.

"The Holy Spirit and the Church." In *Sermons for Today.* Edited by A. H. Chapple. London: Marshall, Morgan and Scott, Ltd., 1968.

"The Child and the Church." In *Children and Conversion.* Edited by C. Ingle. Nashville: Broadman, 1970.

"Blut" (ῥαντίζω). *Theologisches Begriffslexikon zum Neuen Testament.* Wuppertal: Theologischer Verlag Rolf Brockhaus, 1971.

"2 Corinthians." *Broadman Bible Commentary.* Edited by C. J. Allen. Nashville: Broadman, 1971 (12 vols.).

"Taufe" (βαπτίζω). *Theologisches Begriffslexikon zum Neuen Testament.* Wuppertal: Theologischer Verlag Rolf Brockhaus, 1971.

"How Christian Is the Book of Revelation?" In *Reconciliation and Hope. New Testament Essays on Atonement and Eschatology.* Edited by R. Banks. Grand Rapids: Eerdmans, 1974.

"The Clue to the Meaning of Life." In *What Faith Has Meant to Me.* Edited by C. Frazier. Philadelphia: Westminster, 1975.

"Faith and the Parousia." In *Science, Faith and Revelation. Festschrift for Eric Rust.* Nashville: Broadman, 1979.

"John 12:31–32: The Eschatological Significance of the Lifting Up of the Son of Man." In *Studiem zum Text und zur Ethik des Neuen Testaments: Festschrift zum 80 Geburtstag von Heinrich Greeven.* Edited by W. Schrage. Berlin: De Gruyter, 1986.

"Confessing Baptist Identity." In *A Perspective on Baptist Identity.* Edited by D. Slater. London: Mainstream, 1987.

III. Published Lectures and Shorter Works

"Religious History and Eschatology." Norwood Papers, 1. London: Battley Brothers, 1949.

"The Second Coming of Christ." Norwood Papers, 3. London: Battley Brothers, 1951.

"Reflections on the Ecumenical Movement." Living Issues Booklet. London: Baptist Union of Great Britain and Ireland, 1965.

"Evangelizing the Post-Christian Man." Diamond Jubilee Lecture of the London Baptist Preacher's Assoc., 1969.

"Worship and the Sacraments." The Second Holdsworth-Griff Memorial Lecture. Whitley College, Melbourne, Victoria, Australia, 1970.

"The Contribution of the Book of Revelation to the Christian Belief in Immortality." The Drew Lecture on Immortality, 1972.

"The Christological Controversy in the Baptist Union." Rushden, Northants.

IV. Translations

K. Aland. *Did the Early Church Baptize Infants?* London: SCM, 1963.

R. Schnackenburg. *Baptism in the Thought of St. Paul.* Oxford: Basil Blackwell, 1964.

R. Bultmann. *The Gospel of John.* Ed. and supervised, with assistance from R. W. N. Hoare and J. K. Riches. Oxford: Blackwell, 1971.

V. Articles

"The Church and the Child." *The Fraternal* 50 (1943): 9–13.

"The New Testament Doctrine of the End." *Evangelical Quarterly* 16 (1944): 202–18.

"The Eschatology of the Fourth Gospel." *Evangelical Quarterly* 18 (1946): 97–108.

"The Second Coming of Christ." *The Fraternal* 61 (1946): 6–10.

"The Relation of the Fourth Gospel to the Apocalypse." *Evangelical Quarterly* 18 (1946): 173–86.

"The Two Messiahs in the Testaments of the Twelve Patriarchs."

Journal of Theological Studies 48 (1947): 1–12.

"Doctrinal Developments in the Apocrypha and Pseudepigrapha." *Evangelical Quarterly* 19 (1947): 178–95.

"Immortality." *Journal of the Transactions of the Victoria Institute* 79 (1947).

"A Conservative Thinks Again About Daniel." *Baptist Quarterly* 12 (1948): 341–46; 366–71.

"Biblical Eschatology, I: The Interpretation of Prophecy." *Evangelical Quarterly* 20 (1948): 221–29.

"Biblical Eschatology, II: Apocalyptic Literature and the Book of Revelation." *Evangelical Quarterly* 20 (1948): 272–82.

"The Sacraments." *The Fraternal* 70 (1948): 3–7.

"The Second Coming in the Book of Revelation." *Evangelical Quarterly* 23 (1951): 40–45.

"A Century of Eschatological Discussion." *Expository Times* 64 (1953): 312–16.

"The Rise and Fall of the Little Apocalypse Theory." *Expository Times* 64 (1953): 346–49.

"The Minister and His Bible." *The Fraternal* 92 (1954): 11–16.

"Important and Influential Foreign Books: Gloege's *Reich Gottes und Kirche.*" *Expository Times* 66 (1955): 153–55.

"The Church of Scotland and Baptism." *The Fraternal* 99 (1956): 7–10.

"Demythologized Eschatology." *Theology Today* 14 (1957): 61–79.

"The Significance of the Second Coming of Christ." *The Fraternal* 103 (1957): 6–9.

"Das Reich Gottes und die sittliche Forderung Jesu." *Wort und Tat* 12 (1958).

"Gesetz und Geist in die christlichen Lebesfuhrung (Die Ethik des Apostels Paulus). *Wort und Tat* 12 (1958).

"Baptism in the New Testament." *Foundations* 3 (1960): 15–31.

"The Eschatological Discourses of Jesus." *Review and Expositor* 57 (1960): 153–66.

"Nya Testamentets Dapteologi." *Tro och Liv* 6 (1960): 246–50, 268.

"Interpretation av Rom 6.1–11." *Tro och Liv* 7 (1961): 10–21.

"Ecumenical Encounter in Russia." *The Fraternal* 127 (1963).

"The Case Against Infant Baptism." *Christianity Today* 9 (1964): 11–14.

"Baptist Interpretation of the Place of the Child in the Church." *Foundations* 8 (1965): 146–60.

"Church and Child in the New Testament." *Baptist Quarterly* 21 (1966): 206–18.

"Holy Spirit, Baptism, and the Body of Christ." *Review and Expositor* 63 (1966): 177–85.

"Das Christusbild des Neuen Testaments und unsere Verkundigung." *Wort und Tat* 21 (1967).

"I Still Find Infant Baptism Difficult." *Baptist Quarterly* 22 (1967): 225–36.

"The Second Chapter of Colossians." *Review and Expositor* 70 (1973): 469–79.

"Contribution of the Book of Revelation to the Christian Belief in Immortality." *Scottish Journal of Theology* 27 (1974): 76–93.

"New Testament Apocalyptic: A Christological Eschatology." *Review and Expositor* 72 (1975): 317–30.

"The Preparation of the Gospel." *Review and Expositor* 73 (1976): 205–12.

"The Righteousness of God in the History of Israel and the Nations." *Review and Expositor* 73 (1976): 437–50.

"Eschatology in the Gospel of Mark." *Southwestern Journal of Theology* 21 (1978): 37–53.

"The Parousia in Mark." *Review and Expositor* 75 (1978): 565–81.

"The Authority and Justification for Believer's Baptism." *Review and Expositor* 77 (1980): 63–70.

"Faith in the New Testament: A Baptist Perspective." *American Baptist Quarterly* 1 (1982): 137–43.

"The Theology of the Child." *American Baptist Quarterly* 1 (1982): 197–202.

"The Interpretation of Daniel 7." *Catholic Biblical Quarterly* 45 (1983): 44–58.

"Second Thoughts on the Composition of Mark 13." *New Testament Studies* 29 (1983) 414–20.

"John 3:3, 5: Baptism, Spirit and the Kingdom." *Expository Times* 97 (1986): 167–70.

"Jesus and the Kingdom of God." *Baptist Quarterly* 32 (1987): 141–47.

Abbreviations

BBB	Bonner Biblische Beiträge
BFCT	Beiträge für Förderung Christlicher Theologie
BU	Biblische Untersuchungen
BZ	*Biblische Zeitschrift*
BZNTW	Beihefte zur Zeitschrift für die neutestamentliche Wissenschaft
EKKNT	Evangelische-Katholischer Kommentar zum Neuen Testament
ExpTim	*Expository Times*
FRLANT	Forschungen zur Religion und Literatur des Alten und Neuen Testaments
GNB	Good News Bible
HNT	Handbuch zum Neuen Testament
HNTC	Harper's New Testament Commentary
HTKNT	Herders theologischer Kommentar zum Neuen Testament
ICC	International Critical Commentary
JBL	*Journal of Biblical Literature*
JTS	*Journal of Theological Studies*
KEK	Kritische-exegetischer Kommentar über das Neuen Testament
NIGTC	New International Greek Testament Commentary
NovT	*Novum Testamentum*
NTS	*New Testament Studies*
SBT	Studies in Biblical Theology
SNTSMS	Society of New Testament Studies Monograph Series
SUNT	Studien für Umwelt des Neuen Testaments
TDNT	*Theological Dictionary of the New Testament*
WBC	Word Biblical Commentary

THE SIGNIFICANCE OF ESCHATOLOGY IN THE TEACHING OF JESUS

1

Eduard Schweizer
Professor Emeritus of New Testament
University of Zurich

WHEN I STARTED TO LECTURE at the University of Zurich in 1941 I had been taught by Rudolf Bultmann that since Pauline, and a fortiori synoptic, eschatology is fundamentally Jewish, it must be interpreted critically since "we can no longer look for the return of the Son of Man on the clouds of heaven, or hope that the faithful will meet him in the air." I had also learned from Bultmann that "there is in the New Testament the beginning of a demythologizing of eschatology," especially in the Fourth Gospel, which "cancels out any future judgment in the traditional sense."[1]

Even Karl Barth, under whom I had studied in my last year, was not so very different. He spoke of the last day using the image of a table cloth being removed from the festival table, which had always been ready. In 1945 Werner Georg Kümmel published his book *Verheissung und Erfüllung,*[2] in which he

---

1. G. R. Beasley-Murray, *Jesus and the Kingdom of God* (Grand Rapids: Eerdmans, 1985) 338, citing R. Bultmann, *Kerygma and Myth: A Theological Debate,* ed. H. W. Bartsch, trans. R. H. Fuller (London: SPCK, 1953), 116; and G. Bornkamm, R. Bultmann, and F. K. Schumann, *Die christliche Hoffnung und das Problem der Entmythologisierung* (Stuttgart, 1953), 30–31.
2. Zürich: Zwingl-Verlag, 1956. ET *Promise and Fulfillment,* SBT 23, trans. Dorothea Barton (Naperville, Ill.: Alec Allenson, 1957).

challenged these views. Kümmel emphasized the important role that the idea of a future fulfillment played in the teaching of Jesus. He even declared that Jesus had expected the last day to occur within one generation, though he did allow for a period of time between his death and the end of the world.[3] He did not deny Jesus' emphasis on the presence of the kingdom of God in his own acts and words in any way; on the contrary, he considered this emphasis to be the specific center of Jesus' teaching.[4]

As George Beasley-Murray has said, "The real meaning . . . of the nearness of the End is the eschatological significance of the present through the presence of Jesus; that is, it is a reflection of the significance of Jesus himself."[5] Nine years after Kümmel's *Verheissung und Erfüllung,* George Beasley-Murray's book *Jesus and the Future* appeared, in which he referred to Kümmel's work as not yet "adequately recognized in the English-speaking world."[6] Since I had come to know Professor Beasley-Murray as an amiable colleague at the Baptist Theological Seminary in Ruschlikon near Zurich, his book made a challenging impression on my thinking. He spoke of Mark 13 as "the most ancient document of Christianity," fitting "the rest of the eschatological scheme of Jesus"; and Mk 9:1, not exegetically, but dogmatically difficult, was seen as an authentic word of Jesus.[7] His revised understanding of Mark 13 as a collection of different Jesus-traditions in a primitive Christian catechesis and of Mk 9:1 as developed out of Mk 13:30 (originally perhaps referring to the events of A.D. 70) and of Mt 16:28 as a still further development,[8] is, in my view, closer to the truth. While continuing to have questions concerning authenticity, I am still grateful for his emphasis on the significance of a future fulfillment in the coming kingdom of God and I am especially glad to have learned from and to agree with much of what is said concerning the Son of Man in his recent book, *Jesus and the Kingdom*

---

3. Cf., e.g., 17–18, 20–21, 138–39.
4. Cf. 26–29, 98–101.
5. G. R. Beasley-Murray, *Jesus and the Future* (London: Macmillan, 1954) 224.
6. Ibid., 103.
7. Ibid., 226, 246, and 183.
8. Beasley-Murray, *Kingdom,* 323 and 191–93.

of God.[9] Thus, it might be a not unwelcome contribution to this volume honoring my colleague, the cooperation with whom was again so gratifying during the spring term 1980 in Louisville, Kentucky, to discuss once more the topic of eschatology in Jesus' teaching, which is dear to both of us.[10]

Doubtless, this is a subject that poses real problems, and if I am not mistaken, they will become more and more urgent in the near future. Whether Jesus himself expected the final coming of the kingdom of God within his lifetime, or at least within the lifetime of his disciples, is an issue that will prompt continuing discussion. Personally, I doubt it, since Jesus avoids describing the future in any detail or calculating the time of its coming in any way.[11] When he speaks of it, it is always in images, especially in the imagery of a festival meal. Thus, I consider it at least possible that the ardent expectation of the end of the world in the earliest church is responsible for passages like Mk 9:1 and 13:30 or Mt 10:23; however, questions like this one are not really central. The vexing problem is another one. If and when he speaks of a future apocalyptic event that will bring the end of the world, the last judgment, and the final kingdom of God, it is clear that Jesus shared the eschatological concepts of many contemporary Jews, including John the Baptist.

It is equally clear that the message that distinguishes him from all other people is the proclamation of the presence of this kingdom in his words and deeds (Lk 11:20 and 17:20–21).[12] Even if Jesus did speak of a future fulfillment still to come—and it would be difficult to deny that, even granting the authenticity of Mk 9:1 etc. for the sake of argument—would not this be merely a reflection of the expectation of his time? We could easily agree with those who tell us that the fact that Jesus

9. Ibid., 219–29, the arguments for the priority of Lk 12:28 over against Mt 10:32 (225–29) being especially helpful.

10. As the Festschrift for W. G. Kümmel dealt with the same topic of eschatology, I apologize, pressed by various commitments, for not being able to offer a contribution basically different from my article: "Die Bedeutung der Eschatologie für den Glauben bei Jesus," in *Glaube und Eschatologie: Festschrift für Georg Kümmel,* ed. E. Grässer and O. Merk (Tübingen: J.C.B. Mohr, 1985), 277–84.

11. Cf., for instance, G. Klein, "Eschatologie IV," in *Theologische Realenzyklopädie* 10, 273 against Kümmel, *Verheissung,* 21–22, 53–55, 133–34 etc.

12. Cf. all the passages dealt with in Beasley-Murray, *Kingdom,* 71–107.

shared some conceptions or terms with either Jewish or Christian people of the first century A.D. does not disprove their authenticity, as long as they are not contrary to genuine words, conceptions, or tendencies in the preaching of Jesus.[13]

The real issue is whether these conceptions are more important than other shared conceptions of the day, such as the idea of the earth as a kind of flat disc with the sky as a kind of cover overhead. Where do we draw the line between the conceptions of contemporary Judaism (which already reflect the Hellenistic world views) that Jesus shared, but which are considered obsolete today, on the one hand, and conceptions that were either taken over from the Old Testament and (hellenized) Jewish traditions or created in a unique way by Jesus that are central, even indispensable for faith for all time, on the other hand?

Indeed, as Jürgen Moltmann put it, "eine noch nicht völlig ins Bewusstsein gedrungene Verunsicherung und Infragestellung der fundamentalen Voraussetzung der Theologie: der Bibel und des traditionallen Umgangs mit ihr."[14] He illustrates this fact by pointing to the patriarchal structure of the Old Testament faith. If the structure of patriarchal culture is a necessary ingredient for believing in Yahweh, then how could we exempt the institution of slavery? If, however, this culture simply belongs to the circumstances of its time, why is the syncretism of Old Testament faith with that patriarchalism better than the cult of the "Great Mother" in all her forms? And yet, the prophets fight exclusively against this cult and not against that culture.

The questions become explosive when we turn our attention to those who are interpreting the Old and New Testament without what they would view as an obsolete idea of God. Is God merely a human conception conditioned by culture that we can reject without losing any substantial part of the biblical message? Such a challenge comes from atheists, who interpret the

13. E.g., W. G. Kümmel, "Jesusforschung seit 1950," *Theologische Rundschau* 37 (1965–1966): 42–43. Cf. also Kümmel, *Verheissung,* 135–36 and J. D. G. Dunn, "Prophetic 'I'-Sayings and the Jesus Tradition," *NTS* 24 (1978): 175–98.

14. J. Moltmann, "Die Bibel und das Patriarchat," *Evangelische Theologie* 42 (1982): 480–82: ". . . a radical rethinking and requestioning of the fundamental presuppositions of theology (the Bible and the traditions associated with it) has yet to enter completely into the consciousness of modern interpreters."

Bible as a Marxist program that predates Marxism itself;[15] from Marxists, who have no interest at all in either atheism or in theism as a dogmatic decision for either Marxist or Christian believer;[16] or from Christian theologians, for whom Jesus Christ has replaced a God who is dead.[17] The challenge is so serious because these readers of the Bible are themselves so serious in their searching and so close to the prophets and to Jesus himself in their siding with the poor and dying of this world. Some of them are speaking of the death of God "in boundless suffering,"[18] and it would be very un-Christian simply to ignore their questions.

Moltmann's questions have been evoked by a feminist exegesis of Hosea 1–4, in which the author took Gomer's and therefore also the great goddess' part, and by a protest against this approach, which focused on the understanding of the Bible as the Word of God.[19] As long as a historico-critical method is accepted there is no question of disallowing a critical appraisal of the historic conditions under which a text has been written. Furthermore, one is certainly not prohibited from investigating—as far as this is still possible—the psychology of the prophet and of his wife. Such a psychological investigation may even be indicated; however, it cannot replace the reading and the interpreting of the text. It should help one to understand the text of Hosea, not put it aside in order to concentrate solely on its background. We may get the impression that the prophet was not doing justice to his wife and that he was in many ways a strange person. However, was not Ezekiel also a man who did not conform to common standards? And was Paul any different? In all of them, there were repressions and exaggerations and one-sidedness and many other traits that could be considered as negative elements in an average psychology. But the word of God has always been spoken through human beings with good

15. E.g., F. Belo, *Das Markusevangelium marxistisch gelesen* (Stuttgart: Alektor Verlag, 1980).

16. E.g., M. Machovec, *A Marxist Looks at Jesus* (Philadelphia: Fortress, 1976).

17. E.g., D. Sölle, *Stellvertretung* (Stuttgart: Kreuz-Verlag, 1967).

18. Ibid., 12: cf. the whole section 9–12.

19. H. Balz-Cochois, "Gomer oder die Macht der Astarte," *Evangelische Theologie* 42 (1982): 37–65; H. J. Hermission, "Der Rücschritt oder: Wie Jahwe mit Astarte versöhnt werden soll," ibid., 290–94.

and bad sides, with gifts and defects, with successes and short-comings, with all the burden that an average person has to bear. And yet, the church of all centuries has experienced the word of God itself breaking through all these positive and negative factors.

Questioning as an historian or a psychologist why the word of God has taken on this or that form is certainly to be allowed and even recommended. But while whatever we may detect as a historical or (with even more uncertainties) psychological fact can help to understand the word, it cannot replace it. Now, the very contents of Hosea's book are his fights against the cult of the "Great Mother," against the mixture of Yahweh and Astarte, i.e., of God and a divine Nature. We may certainly observe the limits of the imagery, which is a part of his life-setting, as we should always remember the limits of any language. If, however, we confound the message of the prophet with what we may detect of the psychological conditions of Hosea or even Gomer, it is no longer interpretation of the text.[20] This would be equivalent to letting the Palestinian or Hellenistic conceptions of Jesus or of Paul replace their messages. I certainly admit that the task of separating the message itself from the form in which it is delivered is a very difficult one and needs some subtlety. Yet, if the task of the exegete is not hopeless, it must at least be possible to see the main point of the author we are reading.

This does not mean that we should be blind to all one-sided images or statements of a male-determined culture in the Bible. Yahweh is mother as well as father, and Israel is comforted by him "as one whom his mother comforts" (Isa 66:13, etc.); and the golden calf of Ex 32:4 is in Hebrew as well as Greek definitely male. The male gender of the Lord certainly does not justify any "masculinism." As long as we do not delete all the female traits of Yahweh in the Bible or overlook the condemnation of the golden male calf, let alone the strangely passive figure of the suffering Jesus, we cannot dream of any idea of a divine male being endorsed by the Bible. Conversely, these biblical findings

20. Even more is this true of Jesus, in whose psychology the New Testament authors were not much interested, as it seems, even less so than in the historical dates of his biography. This is the difficulty in Hanna Wolff's book, *Jesus der Mann* (Stuttgart: Radius-Verlag, 1977).

simply cannot be used as the foundations of "feminism." But it does mean that any syncretism of a belief in the Lord with a cult of Nature, of our own history, efficiency, or creativity, of male or female sexuality is clearly and definitely rejected. The severity of this rejection is not to be softened by the legitimate observation that it is expressed in a language shaped by the culture, the experiences, and the total circumstances of the life of its author, as is true of any statement of the Bible. Even if the language of the prophet Hosea is particularly foreign to us and perhaps explicable by some psychological insights of today, it does not annul the binding force of what he tries to tell us as the word of God. He may have been unjust to his wife, and he is certainly a sinner as any other biblical author, but whether or not he is more so than the others is not really a matter for our investigation.

Even more burning is the question whether speaking of God might simply be conditioned by the culture and the world view of a bygone day. God-language may not be as strange and foreign as some passages in Hosea. It may not be earmarked for psychological analysis in the same degree as Hosea's stories. It may rather be considered as a general view shared by a majority of men, at least in former centuries. And yet, all this does not exclude the possibility of its being an illusion, time-honored though it may be. Could it not belong to the presuppositions of a past time and not to the word itself, which we have to interpret and to proclaim?

Dorothee Sölle's pleading for a faith in which Jesus has become the definitive representative of the dead God in a "posttheistic" time and culture is tempting. But if Jesus has taken over the role of God for people of today, if the "resurrection" of God is dependent on people, who will build in obedience to Jesus' visions a new society in which every person finds his or her identity? In such a view, is Jesus more than a consul general whose country has ceased to exist? He may then keep up appearances, he may hope that his country will rise again, but he is actually without any authority and power and can only hope for the achievements of people following him.[21]

21. Cf. E. Schweizer, "Jesusdarstellungen und Christologien seit Rudolf Bultmann," in *Rudolf Bultmanns Werk und Wirkung*, ed. B. Jaspert, (Darmstadt: Wissenschaftliche Buchgesellschaft, 1984) 125–26; idem, "Jesus Christus," forthcoming in *Theologische Realenzyklopadie*.

It is true that there is no explicit theology in Jesus' preaching; God is not the object of his teaching. However, the same is true for Christology or pneumatology. And yet, it is nothing else than the life of God and of his Spirit that expresses itself in Jesus' life, acts, and words and makes them the life, acts, and words of the Christ. There is no doubt that his whole existence was directed towards God. This can be explicit in words like Mk 10:18 ("Nobody is good except the one God") or in his prayer ("Abba" in Mk 14:36, "Father" in Lk 11:2). It is expressed implicitly in his parables, for instance, in the parable of the merciful father (Lk 15:11–32), and in his life as a servant, his suffering and dying, always open to the way and will of his heavenly Father. Without that dimension, without his total openness to the living God, Jesus' words and deeds, his passion and his death, not to mention his resurrection (which is in the earliest texts his "being raised"), would become totally alienated from what they are in the Gospels.

It is no different in the post-Easter kerygma. Again, it is true that we do not find an explicit theology in Paul's letters, not because the existence, life, and importance of God are in question for the apostle, but because they are the unquestionable presuppositions of all his writing. Wherever this is not the case, in the world of paganism, for instance, Paul states the fundamental difference: "When you did not know God, you were in bondage to beings that by nature are no gods; but now that you have come to know God . . ." (Gal 4:8–9, cf. 1 Thes 4:5). Therefore, when addressing himself to former Gentiles the belief in God becomes an explicit item in confessional formulae or summaries: "There is one God, the Father, from whom are all things and for whom we exist, and one Lord Jesus Christ, through whom are all things and through whom we exist" (1 Cor 8:6, cf. 1 Thes 1:9).[22] This shows how fatal it would be to interpret the lack of explicit statements about indubitable presuppositions as a sign of their relative insignificance in which they are understood as an elective rather than the compulsory element of belief.

---

22. Cf. E. Grässer, "Ein einziger ist Gott," in *Ich will euer Gott werden,* SBS 100 (Stuttgart, 1981), 179–80, 184–85, and F. Hahn, "Die Schöpfungsmittlerschaft Christi bei Paulus und in den Deuteropaulinen," in *Parola E. Spirito, Festschrift S. Cipriani* (Brescia: Paideia, 1982) 665.

When we now turn to the problem of eschatology the questions are much the same. The early confessional formula in 1 Cor 15:3–5 does not say anything about an eschatological hope. And yet, the very center of the formula "died for our sins" is senseless without the expectation of a last judgment in which all will have to answer for their lives in the presence of God. Thus, again the conviction of a coming final assessment by God is presupposed and not mentioned explicitly because it goes without saying.

The Aramaic acclamation *Maranatha* may have called originally for the exalted Lord to enter the assembled church of his followers in order to judge the sinner.[23] In all three passages (1 Cor 16:22; Did 10:6; and, in Greek translation, Rev 22:20), *Maranatha* follows a statement that draws a separating line between the sinner and the community of the holy ones. However, even if this might be true, it would be an anticipation of the final coming of the judge at his parousia. Whether the acclamation is focused on a present intervention or is an expression of the church's longing for the final fulfillment, it is not a confessional formula but a call that presupposes the belief in the parousia of Christ.

This is different in the missionary proclamation of Christ. According to 1 Thes 1:9–10 the coming from heaven of the Son is explicitly part of the belief to which the Thessalonians have converted. It stands side by side with believing in a living and true God, and its foundation is God's raising Jesus from the dead. Actually, the soteriological dimension is even connected directly with Jesus' final coming, which will deliver the faithful from the wrath to come. This means that the parousia and the eschatological fulfillment are not part of confessional formulae[24] but are probably always presupposed in them. This might be rather controversial with regard to hymns, which seem to praise a fulfillment that has already been reached, though this is

---

23. Cf. 1 Cor 5:4–5: "When you are assembled, and my spirit is present with the power of our Lord Jesus, you are to deliver this man to Satan . . . "

24. Because they are speaking of the past saving events (H. Conzelmann, "Grundriss der Theologie des Neuen Testaments," *Einfuhrung in die Evangelische Theologie* Bd. 2 [Munich: Leaiser, 1968, 1976] 88).

not as evident as it is usually considered. The aorist of the last line in 1 Tim 3:16 ("taken up in glory") seems to be final, and yet the church that sings the hymn is actually witnessing the ongoing mission among the nations. The original hymn in Col 1:15–20 speaks of the definitive reconciliation of all things in the resurrected Christ, again in an aorist, but the author of the letter interprets it (in conformity with the singing church?) as a reconciliation in faith that is to continue up to the day on which the believers will be presented holy and blameless and irreproachable before him (the Christ of the parousia).

The goal of Phil 2:6–11 is the bowing of every knee in heaven and on earth and under the earth and the confessing of every tongue that Jesus Christ is Lord. In Paul's understanding this will happen at the parousia, as 1 Cor 15:24–28 shows, as does his quotation of the same prophetic passage as pointing to the last judgment of God in Rom 14:11. Whether this was also the original understanding of the hymn we do not know, though some arguments can be alleged in favor of it.[25] Be this as it may, it is clear that there are very often assumptions that are not articulated and yet are very central to the original author and/or the New Testament writer who incorporates a piece of tradition in his work (or the church singing a hymn or expressing its faith in a traditional formula). Only where they do no longer go without saying, as, for instance, in a missionary situation, are these assumptions explicitly formulated.

In some way, faith is, as Daniel Patte expresses it,[26] much more dependent on underground convictions that impose them-

25. O. Hofius, *Der Christushymnus Phil 2, 6–11,* Wissenschaftliche Untersuchungen zum Neuen Testament 17 (Tübingen: J. C. B. Mohr, 1976) 33–34. Contrariwise, G. B. Caird thought that even Paul himself had changed his view of 1 Cor 15 and had, in the time of the Philippians, believed in a conversion of the powers before the coming of the Christ in the parousia (*Principalities and Powers,* 1956, 27–28). This was important for him because of the consequences for social work (ibid., 28–30). Whether those "under the earth" are really demoniacal powers (who are imagined as living in the air between heaven and earth rather than under the earth) or dead people is not sure at all.

26. D. Patte, *Paul's Faith and the Power of the Gospel: A Structural Introduction to the Pauline Letters* (Philadelphia: Fortress, 1983) 11–12.

selves upon the believer as a self-evident truth than on ideas that can be manipulated by others, strung together in a logical order and buttressed by arguments. This means that we should take all the underlying "taken-for-granteds" even more seriously than the articulated dogmas. According to Patte the really important points are to be seen in the whole existence of a believer rather than in confessions.[27] He tries to apply this rule to the interpretation of original traditions or of the biblical writer and of all the acts of those who read him and live by his message. This may be a bit exaggerated, and it is in some way also moderated by other passages in Patte's book; nonetheless, there is some truth in his statement. Thus, we have to distinguish clearly between details such as the expectation of the final coming of the kingdom of God within one generation on the one hand, and basic convictions that underlie the whole of one's existence, such as the conviction of Jesus that God will redeem all his promises in his future kingdom on the other. "To limit the significance of eschatology in the teaching of Jesus to the individual is to do grave injustice to it, and to threaten the historical character of the gospel."[28]

That there is a fundamental hope for a coming fulfillment in the teaching of Jesus is proved by the parables. The parables certainly do not simply describe, in the way of the wisdom literature, facts that are always and everywhere true. They speak of what becomes true in the words and acts of Jesus in a very surprising and unexpected way. Therefore, there is scarcely one parable without a surprising trait. It is never simply miraculous, rationally impossible, but it is unexpected indeed. What father would wait as patiently and welcome his prodigal son as cordially as the father in Lk 15:11–32?[29] Only the father of whom Jesus speaks. What king would invite gypsies and beggars to the wedding meal of his son? What money-lender would simply strike out the 500 denarii of the debtor (Lk 7:41) or even lend fifty million denarii (equivalent to as many day-wages) as the one in Mt 18:24? What woman would use 100 pounds of flour

27. Ibid., 14.
28. Beasley-Murray, *Kingdom,* 339.
29. Beasley-Murray, ibid., 114–15, emphasizes the fact that the love of this father becomes true in Jesus.

(Lk 13:21)? What farmer would tell in great detail of all his fail-ures[30] without grumbling, even praising the rich harvest as the one in Mk 4:3-9? What mustard seed grows into a tree (Lk 13:19)?[31] The first three of these examples show how definitely Jesus is convinced that God himself is really acting in his words and deeds, the last three how much he is also convinced that God will unerringly fulfill what has started now.[32]

The same is true in a more general way when we turn to the whole way of Jesus. When he invited tax collectors to his table he was certainly sure of God's validating the new relation of these men to his kingdom. Forgiveness had already happened in this new fellowship. And yet, the Beatitudes clearly show that the glory promised to the poor and suffering ones that are open to listen to Jesus' words is a future one. God will validate what Jesus proclaims.[33]

Even more important is Jesus' journey to Jerusalem. One may be more critical of the authenticity of the predictions of his suf-fering than George Beasley-Murray;[34] it would be difficult, however, to exclude the probability of Jesus' reckoning with at least the possibility of violent death in the holy city. Whatever his consciousness of an imminent death may have been, he cer-tainly went to Jerusalem with the conviction that the will of God, the fulfillment of what God had planned within and be-yond his own earthly existence, was *the* goal. Therefore, he chal-lenged his opponents enormously by the prophetic sign of the cleansing of the temple. Moreover, he gave himself totally into the hands of his Father when eating the Last Supper with his disciples.[35] Therefore, the last cry of desolation on the cross was still directed to "my God." How much or how little pas-sages like Wisdom 2-5[36] may have been in the mind of Jesus,

30. Italics in original; ibid., 197.
31. Observed also ibid., 194.
32. Cf. ibid., 195: "The unity of the beginning and the end of God's sovereign intervention is axiomatic"; also *Future,* 183-84.
33. Beasley-Murray, *Kingdom,* 162.
34. Ibid., 237-47.
35. I agree with G. R. Beasley-Murray in considering the words of Jesus at the Last Supper, especially in their Pauline form, as being close to what he himself said (ibid., 265-67) and did (Schurmann's argu-ment of the *ipsissima facta* of Jesus' "gift-gesture" (ibid., 268-73).
36. Cf. ibid., 241-42.

he certainly was always open to the future of God and, as far as the traditions show, even more so on the last evening and even on the cross. Thus, his whole life was in some way directed towards his validation by God's act of the resurrection.[37]

We then may say indeed that predictions like Mk 13:24–27 are not "steno-symbols" with one-to-one meanings (as in a language of science and logic), but "tensive symbols," open language that reflects the struggle that belongs to organic life (as in poetry and liturgy), and that this is also true for the conglomeration of mythic symbols, for instance, in Revelation. An account of the parousia cannot, therefore, be produced from either Mark 13 or Rev 19:16ff, as little as an account of the birth, life, death, and resurrection of Jesus could be produced from Revelation 12.[38] And yet, the coming parousia of Jesus Christ is the goal without which his life and death and resurrection would be void; for, in the New Testament, it is the great feast of God for the world, much more so than the Dies Irae.[39] The waiting for it, the hope of the church for the consummation of the kingdom of God as represented in Jesus' life, death, and resurrection, is the way in which faith is living in the period between Easter and Parousia. "The ultimate meaning of the parousia is the light it casts on the significance of Jesus, appointed as Christ and Son of Man for the accomplishment of the divine will in the saving sovereignty that we call the kingdom of God . . . alike in its initiation in his ministry, in its powerful 'coming' in the cross and resurrection, and in its consummation in the parousia."[40]

37. Cf. Wolfhart Pannenberg, *Gründzuge der Christologie,* (Gütersloh: Gütersloher Verlagshaus Geerd Mohn, 1964) 60. ET *Jesus—God and Man,* trans. L. Wilkins and D. Priebe (Philadelphia: Westminster, 1968).

38. Cf. Beasley-Murray's reference to N. Perrin's terminology and his review of Perrin's position in *Kingdom,* 339–42.

39. Ibid., 342.

40. Ibid., 344.

APOCALYPTIC, LITERACY, AND
THE CANONICAL TRADITION

2

Ronald E. Clements
Professor of Old Testament Studies
King's College
University of London

THERE OCCURS IN Mk 13:14 a brief clause amounting to no more than three words which have had, in spite of their brevity, a considerable impact upon the study of biblical eschatology. Not least they proved to be of considerable importance to Dr. G. R. Beasley-Murray's early and still profoundly significant study of Mark 13 and of Jesus' expectations for the future.[1] The words are: ὁ ἀναγινώσκων νοείτω, "Let the one who reads understand." In his early (1864) study of the messianic hope of Jesus, the Strasbourg scholar T. Colani found in these words evidence that the "Little Apocalypse" of Mark 13 was based on an earlier written text which had come to be incorporated into the Gospel tradition and to be understood as the teaching of Jesus. The short rubric to the reader betrayed the fact that an already extant written document lay at the back of the Gospel report of the eschatological teaching of Jesus. A considerable number of

---

1. G. R. Beasley-Murray, *Jesus and the Future* (London: Macmillan, 1956). Cf. also idem, *A Commentary on Mark 13* (London: Macmillan, 1957). The purpose of drawing attention back to these much discussed words at this time is especially a mark of this writer's own deep indebtedness to George Beasley-Murray for the stimulus he has given to us over the years to maintain a deep and lasting love of the Bible. Not least has been his modelling a deep respect of the value and importance of scholarly research as a true expression of that love.

scholars took up this view that the phrase did reflect the prior existence of a written eschatological discourse, several of them suggesting that it may have been a Jewish apocalyptic text that had been adapted to the Christian message.

However, since the substantial part of Mk 13:14 makes reference to τὸ βδέλυγμα τῆς ἐρημώσεως, "the sacrilege that makes desolate," with its connections with Dan 9:27, 11:31, and 12:11, it may also be contended that the purport of the short rubric to the *reader* to take careful note was to draw attention to connection with these other scriptural passages.[2] It could then be understood to be a device to alert the reader to the special significance of the pronouncement regarding the desolating sacrilege as marking an event already foretold in earlier Scripture as a sign of the end time. Both possibilities need certainly to be considered and are not wholly exclusive of each other. The written form of the apocalyptic discourse of Jesus is then coupled with earlier written prophecy from the Old Testament.

G. R. Beasley-Murray is sharply critical of the argument that the address to the reader provides evidence of an already extant apocalyptic document. He comments: "More than any other single factor it has given rise to the view that the unknown apocalyptic writer has here nodded, forgetting that such an exhortation is inappropriate in the mouth of Jesus *speaking* (so Colani and a multitude of followers)" (G. R. Beasley-Murray, *A Commentary on Mark 13*, London, 1957, p. 57). Elsewhere he had earlier written, "It would be hard to find in the whole New Testament a better case than this for adducing the hypothesis of gloss!" (idem, *Jesus and the Future*, London, 1956, p. 18). Since the Markan evangelist does himself introduce a number of comments and interpretations for the reader (e.g., Mk 5:41; 7:3, 11, 19), it certainly cannot be ruled out that the comment is the work of the Gospel writer designed to assist in the understanding of the teaching that he conveys. However, the issue concerning at what stage this short note was introduced into the text is

2. Cf. V. Taylor, *The Gospel According to St. Mark* (London: Macmillan, 1952) 511f. Taylor comments: "Alternatively, and perhaps more probably, it is interpreted as a pointed allusion to the Book of Daniel made explicit in Mt. xxiv:15" (p. 511). He goes on to suggest that more than this was intended and that the allusion is made in this cryptic fashion because anything more precise would have been politically dangerous.

one that cannot be resolved with more than varying degrees of probability, whether the evangelist himself introduced it or a later scribe. That the intention is to draw the reader's eye to recognize the special import of the message contained in the verse and the allusions that it contains to earlier passages of Scripture in the book of Daniel and elsewhere in the writings of the Old Testament would appear to be highly likely.

Besides the possibility that the gloss, if it be such, draws attention to the wider scriptural context in which the words of Jesus are to be understood, it also raises two further issues that have assumed growing importance to biblical scholarship. The first of these concerns the importance of literacy, and of the implications of literacy, for the interpretation of the biblical tradition. The second concerns the relevance that such a phrase has within the frame of reference of what has come to be described as "canon criticism."

As far as the first point is concerned it should certainly be borne in mind that the earliest Christian communities were only semi-literate and that many of them almost certainly contained only a small proportion of fully skilled and literate leaders and teachers. Among the Galilean and Judean communities to which the teaching of Jesus was first made known, it is probable that the degree of literacy that prevailed was not particularly high. Even those who could write may often have attained only a limited skill in doing so; thus their habits of mind and conventions of practice were those that belonged to a society in which information was largely conveyed orally. That the skill of the fully literate scribe was still something of a rarity made his expertise of great value to the early Christian churches, where the reading, copying, and interpretation of Scripture came to be held in very high regard. If this were the case, and it is highly probable, even though we lack precise statistics to ascertain the details, then it is necessary to understand this brief comment to the reader in Mark's Gospel in the light of it. What the illiterate person cannot fully understand because of his or her inability to perceive the connections with earlier scriptural passages the literate person can pursue with greater skill. The comment therefore cannot be regarded as a relatively minor and unimportant one, but as a serious and necessary pointer to the deeper significance of the teaching that has been given.

It is noteworthy that in the initial stages of the form criticism of the Gospel tradition attention was drawn most fully to those characteristics that reflected forms of oral teaching and communication.[3] The more recent development of redaction criticism has naturally served to complement this by paying more attention to the written nature of the Gospels as texts. Even so, at least in their early development, the transition from orality to literacy has been considered primarily from the perspective of accurate preservation.[4] Undoubtedly written formulation of the Christian message and teaching, once the church had spread throughout the Roman Empire, became a matter of key importance to the preservation of its integrity. The difference between orality and literacy, however, is far more than a difference in the manner and reliability of the preservation of important material. "Writing restructures consciousness," claims Walter Ong,[5] and certainly the many studies that have been devoted to the impact of literacy upon the way people think bears this out.[6] The very nature of language, the use of repetition and figures of speech, and the way in which words and verbal images are related to ideas are all deeply affected by written preservation. Writing not only provides a more fixed and durable mode of disseminating truths, avoiding the pitfalls of a continued series of subtle changes being introduced, but it enables connections and meaning to be conveyed that would not be readily perceptible to the non-literate mind. There would seem therefore to be little reason for doubting that the short phrase in Mk 13:14 is not an intended, or inadvertent, pointer to the existence of an apocalyptic source document, but a witness to the differences of understanding available to the literate, over against the non-literate, person.[7] The significance of all that is implied by the

3. Cf. R. Bultmann, *The History of the Synoptic Tradition,* trans. J. Marsh (Oxford: Basil Blackwell, 1963).

4. This issue was raised especially by H. Riesenfeld, *The Gospel Tradition and Its Beginnings. A Study in the Limits of 'Formgeschichte'* (London: A.R. Mowbray, 1957).

5. W. J. Ong, *Orality and Literacy. The Technologizing of the Word* (London and New York: Methuen, 1982) 78ff.

6. Cf. esp. J. Goody, *The Domestication of the Savage Mind* (Cambridge: Cambridge University, 1977).

7. This, of course, leaves open the possibility of whether or not there existed an earlier written record of an eschatological discourse from Jesus, as argued most recently by D. Wenham, *The Rediscovery of Jesus' Eschatological Discourse,* Gospel Perspectives 4 (Sheffield: JSOT Press, 1984) esp. 217ff.

reference to "the sacrilege that makes desolate" will only be understood by the person who can *read* the Old Testament Scriptures.

The importance of traditions of textual exegesis current among Jewish rabbis and employed in the exegetical tradition of the synagogue for an understanding of apocalyptic, especially in the book of Revelation, was argued for by A. Schlatter.[8] The deep respect G. R. Beasley-Murray retained for Schlatter's biblical exegesis and his advocacy of it should certainly not pass unremarked; however, it has been very much to the credit of the Swedish scholar Lars Hartman to have shown the importance of this tradition of rabbinical textual exegesis for the interpretation of Mark 13. We may cite Hartman's general position:

> We get a certain idea of how the creative mind of the author worked with the material it had learned when we are able to determine which OT passages are echoed in the text and then consider how it came about that the author recalled these particular passages and why his "intuition" or his exploring mind sought out just this or that passage in the OT.[9]

The development of Jewish apocalyptic was, therefore, very markedly a scribal activity, developed with the aid of written texts and dependent upon the ability of the interpreter to recognize specific allusions and to make certain verbal connections that would not be obvious to the non-literate person. Yet it should certainly not be assumed that the import of what was to be conveyed through these allusions was without interest to such a person. The skilled literate person, well-versed in the art of picking up this complex range of contextual images and ideas, would be expected to explain and assist the less skilled in appreciating their value. It would then appear that it is precisely this situation which has occasioned the rubric to the reader in Mk 13:14. What is being conveyed by the eschatological discourse of Jesus is not simply a prophecy about forthcoming events, but at the same time a vitally significant evaluation of the import and meaning of those events for all who look to the Hebrew Scriptures as the ground and guide of their hope. This

8. A. Schlatter, *Das Alte Testament in der johanneischen Apokalypse*, BFCT 16:6 (Gütersloh, 1912).

9. L. Hartman, *Prophecy Interpreted. The Formation of Some Jewish Apocalyptic Texts and of the Eschatological Discourse of Mark 13 Par.* (Lund: Gleerup, 1966).

fact will become evident to the skilled reader of the Scriptures, especially the book of Daniel, but will need to be explained to the nonexpert who will be unable to achieve this.

I have elsewhere, in the article "Prophecy as Literature: A Re-Appraisal,"[10] drawn attention to the way in which written prophecy differed from the forms of orally delivered prophecy from which it emerged. We may single out three main characteristics of the way in which this difference manifested itself and of the importance of each of them to the rise of apocalyptic literature. The first of these is what we may describe as the formation of paradigms, or patterns, so that prophecy relating to one set of historical circumstances came to be adapted to apply to others. We may cite as an example of this the allusion to the powerlessness of the "rod and staff" of the Assyrians referred to in Isa 10:24–27. The reference is back to Isa 9:4 (Heb. v 3), with its mention of "the day of Midian," but already by way of earlier developments of the "rod and staff" metaphors in Isa 10:5, 15. It must be accepted, therefore, that the "Assyrians" of Isa 10:24 no longer refers to the imperial power of that name but has become a hidden code-name for some later oppressor of Judah.[11] The original situation has been adapted to a later age, probably a very much later one.

The second point is a close development of this since it concerns the removal of the prophecy from its original historical context and its replacement by a larger context, primarily derived from other prophetic texts. The historical context of the original prophecy is set aside so that as it becomes a paradigm of the divine purpose and activity it receives its new context from the body of prophetic literature in which it is set. This does not mean that it loses all historical reference, since it does, in fact, take on the possibility of being applied to a whole series of further historical events. Nonetheless, the uniqueness of the initial historical context is abandoned, and the prophecy or prophetic theme becomes a part of a much wider scheme of divine revelation. In this sense it truly becomes "apocalyptic"; i.e.,

---

10. R. E. Clements, "Prophecy as Literature. A Reappraisal," *Essays in Honor of James Mays* (Atlanta: John Knox, 1986).

11. Cf. O. Kaiser, *Isaiah 1–12,* OTL; trans. J. Bowden (Philadelphia: Westminster, ²1983) 244: "Assyria has become a code name for the world power."

revelatory of a wide segment of the divine purpose. It should be noted, as K. Koch has done,[12] that this development of prophecy often took bizarre and sometimes dangerous directions, but we may still recognize it as a feature that came to be firmly attached to written prophecy. Just as the very nature of a written document made open the possibility of interpretation on the basis of new literary contexts, so was the original historical context and meaning of the prophecy submerged beneath this.

The third feature whereby written prophecy differed from earlier orally spoken prophecy is already evident within the example cited. Words and metaphors, in this case that of the "rod and staff," originating in Isa 9:4 (Heb. v 3), become connectives to provide a multiplicity of meanings. Even more clear in this regard is the development of the "remnant" motif in Isa 10:20–23, where the notion of "remnant" has originated from the name of the prophet's child Shear-jashub in Isa 7:3. This brief section in the book of Isaiah, which in itself so clearly demonstrates the emergence within the prophetic books of techniques of scribal exegesis that were later applied much more freely and extensively in the formation of apocalyptic and other forms of midrash, is of special interest. The reference to the idea of a remnant has occasioned a need to relate this to the threat of a "full end" (Heb. *kalah*) upon all the earth: "For Yahweh, Yahweh of Hosts, will make a full end, as decreed, in the midst of all the earth" (Isa 10:23). This is noteworthy because it is repeated with near verbal exactness in Isa 28:22 and is then taken up as a part of a more intricate picture of the end-time in Dan 9:27. In all three instances great significance is attached to the belief that such destruction has been "decreed" by God through the voice of prophecy. This undoubtedly implies prophecy that had become written down and was, therefore, available for the reader to consult. It is the literary aspect of prophecy that has made possible such a range of further interpretation of it. The question as to where the primary locus of this decree of destruction was to be found is not made completely clear. Probably, since two instances of its development are to be found in the

---

12. K. Koch, *The Prophets, Vol. 2: The Babylonian and Persian Periods,* trans. M. Kohl, (Philadelphia: Fortress, 1983) 202f. Cf. also his earlier study, *The Rediscovery of Apocalyptic,* SBT Second Series 22, trans. M. Kohl (London: SCM, 1972).

book of Isaiah, we should refer to Isa 6:11. Later associations
with the message of Amos may then have encouraged such a development further (cf. Amos 8:2).

The rise of apocalyptic, therefore, was only possible because
prophecy had come to take on a written form. With this written form there was opened up the possibility of new forms of
interpretation based on scribal techniques of word association,
etymologizing and the like. Moreover, the establishing of a written form resulted in a corpus of literature from which further
guidance might be sought. One scripture could be interpreted
with the aid of another scripture, and it was evidently not long
before scribal interpretation gave rise to harmonizations, supple-
mentations, and even more intricate literary connections. The
original historical context, which was recorded in relation to
prophecies, receded into the background. In its place there
emerged the literary context provided by other literature which
quickly took on the character of a literary canon of texts. We
may cite L. Hartman again in regard to the literary background
of the emergence of Jewish apocalyptic texts:

> This authoritative function of the OT was the point of departure
> from which the Scriptures were interpreted and applied in Judaism.
> The reason why I mention this is that the way in which these texts
> use the OT seems to be akin to that in the *midrashim,* partly owing
> to the fact that the *midrashim,* with their *Sitz im Leben* in the rab-
> binical schools and the synagogues, probably contributed in various
> ways to the material worked on by the creative imagination of the au-
> thors and partly owing to the actual technique.[13]

It is not difficult to appreciate that it was chiefly the use of
such scribal techniques that drew together the otherwise very
different interests of apocalyptic speculation and wisdom. Both
depended on the elaboration of subtle literary techniques, such
as the scribes had developed, for an adequate appreciation of
their meaning. Apocalyptic became a form of prophecy intelligible to scribes. Nor is it difficult to see how much of the fas-
cination of such developments, so far as prophecies about the
end-time were concerned, owed not a little to a deep feeling
for the power and mysterious intensity of the written word,

---

13. Cf. J. Z. Smith, "Wisdom and Apocalyptic" in *Visionaries and
their Apocalypses,* Issues in Religion and Theology 2; ed. P. D. Hanson
(London: SPCK, 1983) 101–20. (Hartman, *Prophecy,* 111).

especially among those who were either illiterate or only partially so.

It is this feature of apocalyptic, both in its Jewish and Christian forms, which leads us to the final consideration of the present discussion. The past fifteen or so years of biblical scholarship have witnessed the advocacy of a variety of forms of "canon criticism" as a serious alternative to earlier forms of historico-critical exegesis of the Bible.[14] The range of the discussion and the various ways in which the notion of canon is capable of being understood need not occupy too much of our attention. The discussion has tended, perhaps inevitably, towards discussion of the significance of the range and limits of the biblical canon, both in its Hebrew and Christian forms, and to the weight which should be placed upon ecclesiastical and synagogal authority for the final shape of the canon.

In endeavoring to single out those areas where a substantial basis of reference to the canon can be of greatest assistance to the biblical exegete, two features can be singled out. The first of these is that, over against the very extensive emphasis upon the defining and dating of "sources" within the biblical materials, it is important that the extant form of the biblical books should be fully understood and recognized. The final form of the text does not have to be the only form that concerns us, since it was undoubtedly the end product of a long process; but it is nonetheless the form that has survived for use within both church and synagogue. This undoubtedly meant that, understood from the point of view of a literary meaning of the text, passages of Scripture, and, indeed, all the books of the Bible, were read as continuous wholes. A synchronic reading of the whole was, therefore, the way in which both Jews and Christians understood the text. As far as we can tell from the way in which single authorship came to be ascribed even to such immense literary constructions as the Pentateuch, which was undoubtedly the product of many centuries of scribal activity, this assumption of a synchronic unity gave rise to certain expectations of uniformity of interpretation. This is particularly important when we consider the complex literary composition that modern scholar-

14. Cf. esp. B. S. Childs, *Introduction to the Old Testament as Scripture* (Philadelphia: Fortress, 1979); idem, *The New Testament as Canon. An Introduction,* (Philadelphia: Fortress, 1985).

ship has adduced as the explanation for such a work as the prophecy of Isaiah. We can readily recognize, by the aid of the accumulated insights and research of many generations of critical scholars, that this complexity in respect to text finds its most satisfactory explanation in the assumption of multiple authorship over a long period of time. What is of importance for the modern biblical interpreter for understanding how and why the scholars of antiquity arrived at their interpretations of the text is that they did so from the perspective of very different assumptions. Rightly expecting to find integrity and consistency in the divinely given message, they resorted to subtle harmonizations and to the belief in multiple meanings in particular words and metaphors in a way which the modern reader finds confusing and disturbing. Yet such scribal techniques were in themselves important steps in the direction of establishing meaning in relation to texts that they had come to value very highly.

When we realize the impact of literacy upon the interpretation of prophecy we have found the most important key for understanding how the prophetic literature came to be drawn more and more fully into the new, and very distinct, dimension of apocalyptic. This is, indeed, "prophecy among the scribes"; but in order for the scribes to have had access to the prophecies, the original prophetic word had to be written down. This point is of considerable importance when we consider the question whether apocalyptic began with any coherent and systematized body of doctrines. It appears unlikely that this was the case. Rather, apocalyptic made certain basic assumptions about the divine purpose for Israel, as revealed through prophecy, but came only gradually to develop these assumptions further in the direction of establishing a coherent picture of what the future held in store for Israel and the world. At so many points we discover diversity and flexibility to be the watchwords of an apocalyptic understanding of history. Basic to its understanding was that it needed to identify what had been "decreed" (i.e., revealed through a prophet and preserved in writing for posterity). To this extent literacy was an indispensable tool of interpretation for the apocalyptists.

A further feature of what was implied by the injunction "Let the one who reads understand," also calls for consideration. It is fundamental to the contention set out here that this injunction was concerned to relate the eschatological message of Jesus to the Old Testament Scriptures and in particular to the book of Daniel. The literate person would perceive the connections and links which the non-literate person would be incapable of doing. It may then be argued that this points us to one of the most significant and valuable features of a canonical approach to the Bible. The collection of texts into a corpus and the elevation of this corpus to the status of forming a "canon" implies that one passage may, and indeed should, be read in conjunction with another. To this extent we can discern a very large gulf between the established historico-critical approach to the interpretation of the Bible and the older and more traditional method of "interpreting scripture by scripture." Where the "historical" method seeks to uncover the original circumstances, intentions, and ideas of the author, the "canonical" approach ignores this in favor of regarding the remainder of the canonical Scriptures as forming the true spiritual context.[15]

It is not difficult to perceive that this latter approach can lead to distortions and false understandings, because very dissimilar passages can be brought into conjunction with each other. Purely superficial connections can be adduced through the chance occurrence of words; however, it must also be noted that the historical approach may also lead to difficulties precisely on account of the limitations endemic to the original historical setting. Often, of course, this may not even be known, as is true still today of a host of passages in the prophetic literature of the Old Testament. We can at most conjecture what the original setting was. However, even when the occasion of a prophecy is known, the extent to which the prophet's original situation can be seen to have historical analogies and counterparts in a later age is dependent entirely upon individual opinions. The rather heavy-handed way in which the prophets' denouncements of their contemporary social leadership has been adduced as applicable in the modern age is a case in point. It must be noted, therefore, that the attempts of the scribal apocalyptists to provide for prophecy a larger and more ongoing understanding of its meaning is of genu-

15. The different assumptions and their significance are well discussed in the review of the debate between James Barr and B. S. Childs by Frank Kermode in "Canons," *London Reviews,* ed. N. Spice (London: Chatlo & Windus, 1985) 149–56.

ine interest and exegetical value. It would be wholly regrettable, therefore, if the ideas of interpretation in a canonical context were allowed to be set over against interpretation in a historical context of the kind that so much modern critical work on the Bible has sought to achieve. Each does in its own way express something of the dialogue between the text and its interpreters which is very important to the rich and extensive task of hearing the word of God.

Apocalyptic patterns of biblical interpretation are to be seen not simply narrowly confined to the biblical books of Daniel and Revelation, but quite extensively spread throughout the prophetic literature of the Old Testament, widely present in the biblical interpretations of St. Paul and, most centrally of all, present in the teaching of Jesus. It may then be hoped that the seeming vagaries and excesses of the biblical apocalyptists, which have so often in the history of the Christian church been the target of heavy criticism and even outright rejection by theologians, may be seen not to be so repulsive as they at first appear. They belong by a kind of theological necessity to the processes by which the word of God, originally proclaimed orally, came to be preserved and disseminated for the benefit of later generations. The tasks of preserving in written form, editing, re-appropriating, and re-interpreting the word of God that had been given "once and for all" was in itself a compound process. The separate techniques and aims came to be fused together in the work of the scribe, who became at one and the same time the guardian of the tradition and also its interpreter.[16] That one scripture should be understood in the light of other passages of the same canonical corpus served both as a springboard for the possibilities of ever-new understandings of the word of God and, at the same time, a check and corrective, lest one part of its message should be stressed to the detriment of the whole.

Historically the function of the Bible in Christian worship and

16. The importance of the development of these patterns of scribal interpretation and their presence in the formation of the Old Testament literature as a form of inner-biblical exegesis is discussed by M. Fishbane, *Biblical Interpretation in Ancient Israel* (Oxford: Oxford University, 1985). The interpretation of prophetic materials is dealt with pp. 443ff.

its central importance for the formulation of Christian teaching and the development of Christian spirituality have meant that the Christian faith has provided a major stimulus towards literacy. Only the person who can read can explore the full riches of the Christian message and its biblical heritage. "Let the one who reads understand" has therefore served as a characteristically Christian injunction for the strengthening of faith and the deepening knowledge of God. Whatever the source of its entrance into Mk 13:14, it undoubtedly represents a very illuminating comment on the complexities of biblical apocalyptic and on the demands that its interpretation places upon the Christian scholar. It also indirectly reveals something of the divide that existed between the literate person and the non-literate one in the life of the Christian church. In the modern world those distinctions still continue to apply, so that we are continually indebted to those scholars through whom we have learned to read the Scriptures discerningly.

MATTHEW 12:28/LUKE 11:20 —A WORD OF JESUS?

3

James D. G. Dunn
Professor of Divinity
University of Durham

JUST WHEN THE RENEWED QUEST of the historical Jesus seemed to have lost all its vitality and to have settled back into comfortable generalizations and trite paradoxes, E. P. Sanders, like a latter day Albert Schweitzer, has tossed the apple of discord once again into the circle of New Testament scholars. In his illuminating and provocative treatment of *Jesus and Judaism*[1] he challenges one of the most firmly established of the "accepted results" of the new quest: that the decisive and distinctive feature of Jesus' message was his proclamation of the kingdom of God as already present.[2] Rather, Sanders suggests, it was the expectation of the future, climactic action of God which "dominated and controlled his activity and message and that future event is what primarily defines Jesus' view of 'the kingdom.' "[3] In an impressively honest attempt not to dictate to the evidence, Sanders seeks to be as open to it as possible: he readily affirms that Jesus *also* thought the *power* of God was present;[4] and he is very

1. E. P. Sanders, *Jesus and Judaism,* (Philadelphia: Fortress, 1985).
2. Sanders, *Jesus,* ch 4. Characteristic of this consensus would be the views of E. Käsemann, "The Beginnings of Christian Theology," *New Testament Questions of Today* (London: SCM, 1969) 102; J. Jeremias, *New Testament Theology: The Proclamation of Jesus* (London: SCM, 1971) 102.
3. Sanders, *Jesus,* 154.
4. Ibid., 153.

willing to recognize that one could stretch the meaning of the word and speak of the kingdom "in the sense of God's power, as present and as extended to individuals in the present."[5] But when he looks at what has usually been regarded as the key verse in this connection (Mt 12:28/Lk 11:20) he feels it to be such an uncertain base within the Jesus-tradition that nothing of any weight can be placed upon it.[6]

One of the sharpest challenges offered by Sanders to a large-scale consensus regarding Jesus and the kingdom can thus be focused on this one text—Mt 12:28/Lk 11:20. Sanders' critique is quite sweeping: Mt 12:28/Lk 11:20 is the key example of a misdirected exegesis—

> I regard most of the exegetical efforts of the last decades as proving a negative: analysis of the sayings material does not succeed in giving us a picture of Jesus which is convincing and which answers historically important questions. . . . we cannot, by analysing the sayings material, really know that such passages (as Matt. 12:28) reveal "the particular and decisive character" of Jesus' preaching of the kingdom, nor that "the real meaning of the eschatological preaching" is that the one who will bring salvation in the last days is already present.[7]

> The entire argument about the isolation and significance of this verse (Matt. 12:28) for understanding Jesus' view of his work, it appears to me, depends more on circular reasoning than on anything else.[8]

The challenge is clear, and its detail will become clearer as we proceed: we can have no confidence that Mt 12:28/Lk 11:20 is an accurate expression of anything Jesus may have said on the subject.

It may be appropriate, then, that one of those to whom Sanders addresses his challenge should attempt a reply—if for no other reason than because in my previous analysis of the passage[9] it was the large-scale consensus that here, if anywhere, was a gen-

5. Ibid., 237. Cf. Johannes Weiss's somewhat tortuous wrestling with Mt 12:28 in his classic *Jesus' Proclamation of the Kingdom of God,* ed. R. H. Heirs and D. L. Holland (London: SCM, 1971) 74–79.

6. Sanders, *Jesus,* 133–41

7. Ibid., 133, 139.

8. Ibid., 135.

9. J. D. G. Dunn, *Jesus and the Spirit* (London: SCM, 1975) 44–49, referring particularly to the opening paragraph of §8.2.

uine word of Jesus, a consensus which made any attempt to defend it seem redundant.[10] Sanders has shattered that
consensus. The demand for a sounder demonstration that the
verse does take us back to Jesus' own words can no longer be
denied or ignored.

Jesus the Exorcist—the Fact

In a praiseworthy attempt to free reconstruction of Jesus' ministry from overdependence on the sayings tradition and from
the endless treadmill of debate about disputed texts, Sanders
proposes that such a reconstruction should start with several
facts about Jesus' career "which can be known beyond doubt."
"The almost indisputable facts" he lists start with Jesus' baptism by John the Baptist and Jesus' being a Galilean who preached
and healed, and continue through Jesus' crucifixion outside Jerusalem by the Roman authorities.[11] This list is important for
Sanders' method, since it will become evident that the only sayings material that is likely to commend itself to him are sayings
that make best sense of these facts within a Jewish context and
that help explain Jesus' death and the subsequent emergence of
Christianity. It is this methodology that, for example, deter-
mines Sanders' point of entry into the Jesus-tradition as the fact
that "Jesus engaged in controversy about the temple"—the *fact*
of Jesus' "cleansing" of the temple marries well to the tradition
that Jesus *said* something about the temple's destruction and
about a new temple, and both fit well into the context of Jewish
"restoration eschatology," while at the same time they are
"highly offensive."[12]

Given then that "facts" are so important for Sanders' reconstruction, it is somewhat surprising that he pays so little attention
to Jesus' reputation as an exorcist. He includes under the rubric
of the second fact that Jesus "healed." But here is a case where
we can be a good deal more specific without straying beyond
the limits of "almost indisputable facts."[13] For Jesus' reputa-

10. See, e.g., the emphatic conclusions of N. Perrin, *Rediscovering
the Teaching of Jesus* (London: SCM, 1967) 64–65; E. Grässer, "Zum
Verständnis der Gottesherrischaft," *ZNW* 65 (1974): 7–11.
11. Sanders, *Jesus,* 11.
12. Ibid., chs 1 and 2, referring particularly to p. 76.
13. See also n. 16 below.

tion as a highly successful exorcist must surely be regarded as part of the base-rock historical data concerning Jesus.

The claim can be quickly demonstrated. (a) Jesus' work as an exorcist is well attested in the Synoptics. Exorcisms form the largest single category of healings (4 exorcisms in Mk 1:21–28 par Lk; Mk 5:1–20 par Mt/Lk; Mk 7:24–30 par Mt; Mk 9:14–29 par Mt/Lk). We may note also the summary references in Mk 1:32–34, 39; 3:11; Lk 7:21, and 13:32. Within the synoptic tradition there can be no doubt that Jesus was remembered as a highly successful exorcist. This is all the more striking when we recall that exorcism features surprisingly little in the earliest churches (specifically only in Acts 8:7 and 16:16–18), with no mention made of it in any version of the post-Easter commission (Mt 28:18–20; Lk 24:46–49; Jn 20:21–23; Acts 1:8)—in contrast to the prominence of exorcism in the commissioning of the Twelve during Jesus' ministry (Mk 6:7 par Mt 10:1/Lk 9:1). The churches that cherished the synoptic tradition remembered exorcism as a characteristic feature of Jesus' ministry, presumably because it was so, and not because exorcism was a special Christian concern.

(b) The most common attack on Jesus in non-Christian sources in the first two centuries of Christianity's existence depicted him as a magician or sorcerer who worked his miracles, exorcisms in particular, by trickery and black magic.[14] This can be readily illustrated on the pagan side from Origen (*contra Celsum* 1:6, 68; 2:49) and Irenaeus (*adv. Haer.* 2:32); in each case it is clear that what is in view is Jesus' success as a miracle worker, particularly in casting out demons—sorcery being primarily the power to control and drive out demons by magical incantation. On the Jewish side we may refer simply to Justin (*Dial.* 69:7) and the rabbinic tradition preserved in *bSanh.* 43a, where equivalent charges of magical art and sorcery are levelled at Jesus.[15] Since sorcery, magical incantation, and exorcism are all of a piece in the general view of the time, it is most likely that this Jewish accusation of magic and sorcery is an

14. Cf. W. Horbury, "Christ as brigand in ancient anti-Christian polemic," *Jesus and the Politics of His Day,* ed. E. Bammel and C. F. D. Moule (Cambridge: Cambridge University, 1984) 183–95.

15. Joseph Klausner, *Jesus of Nazareth* (London: Allen & Unwin, 1925) 27–28. J. Maier, *Jesus von Nazareth in der talmudischen Über-*

echo of the earlier charge levelled against Jesus from within Judaism, according to Mk 3:22—'He casts out demons by the prince of demons'—and echoed also in Jn 7:20 and 8:48, 52.[16] Here too, then, is clear indication that in non-Christian circles as well Jesus' reputation as a successful exorcist was firmly established—so firmly established that it could not be denied by opponents, only denigrated.

(c) Not least in significance is the fact that the name of Jesus was used by *others* in exorcism. The principal reason for this, at least initially, would be Jesus' own success as an exorcist. Because he was known to have exercised such effective authority over the demons, other would-be exorcists would be eager to conjure with his name. And so we find Jesus' name being invoked in exorcism both by his own disciples (Lk 10:17, Acts 16:18), and by others beyond the circle of disciples (Mk 9:38; Acts 19:13). Jesus' wider fame in this connection is confirmed by the use of his name in several incantations preserved in the magical papyri (Papyri Graecae Magicae 4:1233, 3020).

We need not labor the point. Jesus' reputation as a successful exorcist is as firmly established as a historical datum as we could hope for. The only obvious explanation for that reputation is that it was born of a ministry in which successful exorcisms were at least a significant part. In other words, here we certainly have what can properly be called "an almost indisputable fact." If then it is the integration of saying with fact which is to weigh so heavily in evaluating items of the sayings tradition, it follows that it is this more fully described fact (Jesus the successful exorcist, not just Jesus the healer) which should provide our point of departure.

lieferung (Darmstadt: Wissenschaft Buchgesellschaft, 1978) argues that the accusation of sorcery was attached to the name of Jesus only later (pp. 219–37); but the evidence of a much more widespread charge of sorcery levelled against Jesus already in the second century needs to be given more weight. Cf. also M. Smith, *Jesus the Magician* (New York: Harper, 1978) ch 4.

16. Sanders agrees: "that Jesus was charged with the practice of magic seems indisputable" (*Jesus,* 166—another "indisputable fact"!; also p. 174).

Jesus the Exorcist—
The Sayings

When we turn to the sayings tradition to see whether it can at any point be integrated into or shed light upon the fact of Jesus the exorcist, we are not disappointed. For within the sayings tradition we find not just one saying of Jesus regarding exorcism but a group of sayings—in point of fact, two groups of sayings: Mk 3:23–29 and the Q material in Mt 12:25–32, 43–45/Lk 11:17–23; 12:10; 11:24–26—amounting to six sayings in all.

	Mark	Q
(1) Beelzebul charge	3:22–26	Mt 12:24–26/Lk 11:15, 17–18
(2) Spirit/finger of God	———	Mt 12:27–28/Lk 11:19–20
(3) Strong man	3:27=Mt 12:29	Lk 11:21–22
(4) He who is not with me	(9:38–40)	Mt 12:30/Lk 11:23
(5) Blasphemy saying	3:28–29/Mt 12:31	Mt 12:32/Lk 12:10
(6) Return of unclean spirit	———	Mt 12:43–45/Lk 11:24–26

A glance at a synopsis is enough to show that behind the triple tradition are two clearly distinct collections that substantially overlap.

(1) The distinctive details of Mark and Q are clearly discernible;[17] but equally clearly both are versions of the same charge—"He casts out demons by Beelzebul, the ruler of demons . . . a kingdom divided against itself. . . ."

(2) This saying is lacking in Mark; the word-for-word agreement of Matthew and Luke ensures that we have a Q version already in Greek, with the issue of whether Q read "Spirit" or "finger" the only matter unresolved.[18]

(3) The divergence between Mark and Q is complete at the verbal level. But again the substance is effectively the same—a strong man must be defeated before his possessions can be plundered.[19]

---

17. That there is a Q version of (1) is generally agreed; see R. Laufen, *Die Doppelüberlieferungen der Logienquelle und des Markusevangeliums*, BBB 54 (Bonn: Hanstein, 1980) 126 and nn. 3 and 4. For the distinctive details see Laufen, 127–29, 133–34.

18. See below n. 24.

19. That Luke has drawn on Q at this point is the best explanation of the divergence; see Laufen, *Doppel*, 84, 130–31. Gospel of Thomas logion 35 looks to be too dependent on the Mk/Mt form of the saying to serve as independent evidence. But note also the echo in Gospel of Thomas logion 21.

(4) The reason why this saying has been attached to the Q version of (3), as appears to be the case, is not at first clear. But it can hardly be accidental that its nearest equivalent in Mark is attached to the episode of the unknown exorcist (Mk 9:38–40).

(5) Again the distinctive outlines of Mark and Q are sufficiently clear. Since the Lukan context is different it may well be that the saying appeared elsewhere in Q, apart from the grouping (1)–(4), (6). Matthew, however, following Mark's lead, has not only incorporated Mk 3:28–29 but, recognizing the Q equivalent, has also interwoven the two versions with good effect.

(6) Q probably rounded off its collection of exorcism sayings at this point with the brief parable about the return of the unclean spirit—the Greek again being almost word-for-word, as with (2) and (4).

Without needing to go into much detail, we can extend our observations and draw some immediate deductions. (a) Only (1) and (3) are linked in *both* groupings (Mark and Q). These may be regarded as the core material to which other sayings were variously attached—by Q or the pre–Q tradition, (2), (4), and (6), and by Mark or the pre-Markan tradition, (5), with Matthew conflating the two and inserting additional material between (5) and (6).

(b) This core grouping, (1) and (3), most probably had been formed at an early stage prior to the composition of Mark and compiling of Q. Mark can hardly have derived his material from the tradition used by Q; the omissions and different versions are too hard to explain on that hypothesis. Nor is it likely that Mark and Q contrived the same ordering of the sayings purely by chance. Since therefore the grouping of (1) and (3) predates both Mark and Q, and since the detail of the material has diverged in the period between the initial grouping and its use by Mark and Q, the initial grouping of (1) and (3) must have taken place at a very early stage of the tradition history of the sayings.

(c) Moreover, Mark has "topped and tailed" the collections (Mk 3:20–21, 30, also 31–35), which may well indicate that (1), (3), and (5) were already grouped in the pre-Markan tradition before Mark made use of it. In other words, the addition of (5) to (1) and (3) may be regarded as a second stage in the formation of the Markan collection. Likewise in Q, since (1), (3), and (6) form a natural progression (third person analysis of exorcism, its rationale, technique, and possible consequence), which the more directly challenging first person language of **(2)** and **(4)** seems to disrupt, it is quite likely that the grouping of **(1)**, **(3)**, and **(6)** also took place prior to the formation of Q. In other words, here too we may be able to discern a second stage in the tradition history of the Q collection, with Q inserting **(2)** and **(4)** at a third stage in the process, and possibly adding also Lk 11:14/Mt 12:22–23 to introduce the whole collection.[20]

(d) Of these other sayings in Q, **(2)** obviously belongs in an exorcism context. But so also does **(4)**: not only is it sandwiched between the two exorcism passages, **(3)** and **(6)**; but also the clear implication of Mk 9:38–40 and Mt 12:29–30/Lk 11:21–23 is that a controlling consideration in the use of this saying, **(4)**, quite apart from Q, was the awareness that it had to do with Jesus' ministry as an exorcist. The original context of **(5)** is less clear in view of its placement elsewhere in Q. However, it is easy to see why Q should have inserted it at that point (assuming that Lk 12:8–12 follows the order of Q). So even if **(5)** was original, independent of **(1)** and **(3)** we may still consider it very likely that Mark or the pre-Markan tradition was right to link **(5)** into an exorcism context (see also n. 27 below).

(e) It is very likely that the divergence between the Mark and Q versions goes back to the Aramaic stage of the tradition: the material has a strongly Jewish stamp (particularly "Beelzebul" and "the Satan"); and it is most probable that the divergence between Mark and Q at **(5)** is the result of different renderings of ambiguous Aramaic—Mark's rendering reflecting a very early stage before the Aramaic *bar ʾenasa* (= "the son of man") had become formalized into a title ("the Son of Man").[21]

The most obvious explanation for all this is that there was in the earliest Christian congregations a widespread tradition that Jesus had spoken about his ministry of exorcism. The diverse

---

20. Cf. S. Schultz, *Q. Die Spruchquelle der Evangelisten.* (Zürich: Theologisches Verlag, 1972) 206–7. See further below n. 31.

21. See further Dunn, *Jesus,* 49–52; I. H. Marshall, *Luke,* NIGTC (Exeter: Paternoster, 1978) 516–19. M. E. Boring, *Sayings of the Risen Jesus,* SNTSMS 46 (Cambridge: Cambridge University, 1982) 159–64, argues for the saying's origin as an early prophetic utterance (though he allows that Mk 3:28 may go back to Jesus). In so doing he fails (p. 263 n. 18) to take the force of my critique ("Prophetic 'I'-Sayings and the Jesus Tradition: The Importance of Testing Prophetic Utterances within Early Christianity," *NTS* 24 [1977–78]: 175–98) of his own earlier treat-

groupings and details show that the tradition was put to considerable use, but also that underlying the tradition was a shared memory of what Jesus had said, a memory whose outline and substance were clear and common and complementary among the different churches who would have acknowledged the Mark and Q traditions as theirs.

When we marry the findings of this brief sayings analysis to the *fact* of Jesus the exorcist, a coherent and convincing picture emerges. On one or more occasions Jesus spoke about his exorcisms and his words were remembered. This is just as we might expect. Once we grant that Jesus was a successful exorcist, it must also be considered highly probable that Jesus would have been asked about the secret of his success. The stories of ancient exorcisms reveal a wholly natural human curiosity, common to all generations, regarding the reason for and techniques of such success. And if Jesus' technique was unusual (see below), it is all the more likely that he would have been questioned about it. Since his reputation as a successful exorcist was one of the few things that would be widely known about Jesus, it would be surprising if the first Christians did not make a point of remembering how Jesus had replied to such questions, and fully expected that they should use Jesus' own answers when they bore testimony to Jesus on this point on their own account.

In short, Mt 12:28/Lk 11:20 belongs to a sayings tradition which in substance and effect should almost certainly be associated closely with the fact of Jesus' success as an exorcist and traced back to Jesus himself.

---

ment ("How May We Recognize Oracles of Early Christian Prophets in the Synoptic Tradition? Mark 3:28–29 as a Test Case," *JBL* 91 [1972]: 501–12): Given that prophetic utterances would be tested in the earliest Christian congregations before being accepted as words of Jesus, and given that an increasingly high and more explicit Christology would almost certainly be one of the tests used, it follows that any prophecy which treated lightly criticism of Jesus was hardly likely to gain acceptance as a word of Jesus (cf. 1 Cor 12:3). It is not in the nature of charismatic movements to accept criticisms of the charismatic founder *and* to include them among his revered sayings!

Mt 12:28/Lk 11:20—The Criterion
of Double Dissimilarity

Within the Q groupings of sayings, Mt 12:27–28/Lk 11:19–20 has been inserted between (1) and (3). Does this fact signify that Mt 12:28/Lk 11:20 is of later origin, or simply that it was at first remembered independently of (1) and (3)? Is the case for referring it back to Jesus himself so weak and circular as Sanders suggests?

Mt 12:28	Lk 11:20
But if it is by the Spirit of God that I cast out demons, then the kingdom of God has come to you.	But if it is by the finger of God that I cast out demons, then the kingdom of God has come to you.

(a) Sanders makes a great play with the tension between vv 27 and 28 in Mt 12. The problem he sees, as others have before him, is that v 27 likens Jesus' exorcisms to those of other Jewish exorcists, whereas v 28 is normally taken as a claim for the distinctiveness of Jesus' exorcisms. But if Jesus' exorcisms proved that the kingdom of God had come, then the exorcisms of contemporary Jewish exorcists must prove the same. The circularity of which Sanders makes accusation arises from the presumption that Jesus *must* have been conscious of unique power (v 28) and *could not* have ascribed the same power to others (despite v 27).[22]

In so arguing, however, Sanders and the others before him have missed the points of emphasis in the saying. The structure of Mt 12:28/Lk 11:20 places the emphasis on two phrases—

---

22. Sanders, *Jesus,* 134–35, referring particularly to R. Bultmann, *The History of the Synoptic Tradition* (Oxford: Basil Blackwell, 1963) 14, 162; W. G. Kümmel, *Promise and Fulfillment* (London: SCM, 1961) 105–6. See also e.g., T. Lorenzmeier, "Zum Logion Mt 12:28; Lk 11:20," *Neues Testament und christliche Existenz,* Festschrift for Herbert Braun, ed. H. D. Betz and L. Schottroff (Tübingen: J. C. B. Mohr, 1973) 293; H. Schurmann, *Gottes Reich—Jesu Geschick* (Freiburg: Herder, 1983) 106 (this section is a reprint of Schurmann's "Das Zeugnis der Redenquelle für die Basileia-Verkundigung Jesu," in *Logia: Les Paroles de Jésus,* ed. J. Delobel [Leuven: University, 1982] here p. 155). For the strong consensus in German scholarship in favor of the authenticity of Mt 12:28/Lk 11:20 as a word of the historical Jesus, see Laufen, *Doppel,* 439 n. 107, and for those who hold it to be originally independent of the preceding verse see p. 446 n. 162.

"Spirit/finger of God" and "the kingdom of God." We ought in fact to translate thus: "Since it is by *the Spirit/finger* of God that I cast out demons, then has come to you *the kingdom* of God." This means that in the immediate context there is intended a clear distinction between v 27 and v 28. According to v 27 Jesus likens his exorcisms to those of other exorcists, in a very effective *ad hominem* argument; but then he goes on to highlight the distinctive features of his exorcisms. These distinctive features are brought into focus in the two emphasized phrases: he exorcizes by the Spirit/finger of God, and it is this feature of his exorcisms which shows them to be manifestations of the kingly rule of God already in operation, already impacting on those present.[23]

The indicator of the kingdom then is not Jesus' exorcisms as such, but the power to which his exorcisms were attributed. If "Spirit" is original, the utterance in effect lays claim to the Spirit whose outpouring would mark the new age (e.g., Isa 32:15; 61:1; Ezk 37:14; Joel 2:28–29).[24] If "finger" is original, as most surmise, an allusion to Ex 8:19 would be self-evident[25]—the confession of Pharaoh's magicians that Moses' miracles were wrought by "the finger of God." Indeed, in that case we may suppose a play on the already current traditions regarding Jannes and Jambres, the names given to Pharaoh's magicians. According to Ex 7:11, 22, and 8:7 they managed to mimic the first three of Moses' miracles before admitting defeat. And according to CD 5:18–19 (cf. 2 Tim 3:8–9) the source of their oppo-

---

23. J. C. O'Neill, *Messiah* (Cambridge: Cochrane, 1980) also misses the point (pp. 14–15): since the exorcisms are affected by God's eschatological power, it is *they* which have brought the kingdom of God into the presence of the critical onlookers, whatever they think about the exorcisms (cf. Mk 3:29 pars).

24. Because Luke has a clear Exodus typology, seems to avoid attributing healing miracles to the Spirit, and at least once elsewhere sacrifices a Q spirit reference (Lk 20:42), the case for regarding the "Spirit" as original rather than "finger" is stronger than has usually been appreciated; see further Dunn, *Jesus,* 45–46; also Marshall, *Luke,* 475–76; J. M. van Cangn, " 'Par l'esprit de Dieu—par le doigt de Dieu,' Mt 12:28 par. Lc 11:20," *Logia: Les Paroles de Jésus,* 337–42.

25. See particularly T. W. Manson, *The Teaching of Jesus* (Cambridge: Cambridge University, 1931) 82–83.

sition to Moses was Satan (Belial).[26] The charge laid against Jesus therefore attributed to him the role of Jannes and Jambres—his exorcisms effected by Satan as against those of Moses' followers.[27] Jesus responds by taking up the subsequent confession of Egyptian magicians, that Moses acted by "the finger of God," that is, by the incomparable power of God with which they could not compete. The claim to an action of epochal significance equivalent to the deliverance from Egypt would have been implicit (cf. Dan 3:10).[28] Either way then, according to this saying Jesus laid claim to be acting by the eschatological power of God.[29] It is precisely this interconnection of exorcism and eschatology which marks out the speaker of Mt 12:28/Lk 11:20 from his contemporaries, a point recognized by *whomever* prefaced Mt 12:28/Lk 11:20 with Mt 12:27/Lk 11:19 in the first place.[30]

(b) At this point the argument for regarding Mt 12:28 as a word of Jesus does not really depend on assuming either the independence of v 28 from v 27 or their association from the first.[31] For v 28 in itself is enough to highlight the distinctive-

26. See further A. Pietersma and R. T. Lutz in J. H. Charlesworth, ed., *Old Testament Pseudepigrapha,* 2 vols. (London: Darton, 1985) 2:427–29.

27. If this train of thought is indeed implicit, it provides an important link to the blasphemy saying (5).

28. There may be an eschatological implication in the accusation also, since magic or wonders wrought by a fallen or opposing heavenly power were probably regarded as part of Satan's tactic to delay or defeat the age to come (cf. Mk 13:22; 2 Thes 2:9–12; Rev 13:13–15; Pseudo-Philo 60:3).

29. Another obvious parallel would be Saul versus David, bearing in mind that David, upon whom the Spirit of the Lord had come mightily (1 Sam 16:13), in effect acted as exorcist to deliver Saul from the evil spirit which tormented Saul (1 Sam 16:14–23). To be acting in the part of David as against Saul would have obvious messianic significance (cf. Pseudo-Philo 60:3).

30. Cf. Schultz, Q 211–12; Gerd Theissen, *Miracle Stories of the Early Christian Tradition* (Edinburgh: T. & T. Clark, 1983) 277–80: "Nowhere else do we find miracles performed by an earthly charismatic which purport to be the end of the old world and the beginning of the new" (p. 279).

31. It is not possible to reach a clearer verdict on the precise course of the tradition history of the association of these two verses. The chief alternatives are: (1) the sequence (vv 27–28) or v 28 alone belonged with the Beelzebub controversy from the beginning (cf. A. Polag,

ness of Jesus' exorcistic practice. According to v 28, Jesus attributed his success as an exorcist solely to the eschatological power of God working through him. But typical of exorcistic practice in the ancient world was the use of physical aids (e.g., Tobit 8:2—burning the heart and liver of a fish; Josephus, *Ant.* 8:45-49—smell of a root; magical papyri—amulets) and the invocation of some authority power source ("I adjure you by . . ."—as in Acts 19:13). The immediacy of power and authority expressed in Mt 12:28 stands in rather striking contrast.[32] And here again saying meshes very well with fact. For according to the accounts of Jesus' exorcisms, Jesus used no aids and no incantations or formulae of incantation. Rather, the pattern regularly recalled within the synoptic tradition is of nothing more than a simple command—where the words are recorded they usually take the form, "Come out of him" (Mk 1:25/Lk 5:8; 9:25). Thus, whether v 28 was originally independent of v 27 or not, the verse expresses a claim to exercise the eschatological power of God with an immediacy and directness that is borne out by the accounts of Jesus' exorcisms and which effectively distinguish Jesus' exorcistic technique from the practice of his Jewish contemporaries.[33]

Die Christologie der Logienquelle, WMANT 45 [Neukirchen, 1977] 40–41; J. Fitzmyer, *Luke,* AB 28A [New York: Doubleday, 1981 and 1985] 2:918); but why then did Mark not know of or use it? (2) The sequence belonged to another similar but different exchange between Jesus and onlookers, or contains a different reply to a more widespread charge against Jesus (cf. D. Zeller, "Redaktionsprozesse und wechselnder 'Sitz im Leben' beim Q-Material," *Logia: Les Paroles de Jésus,* 406); hypothesizing near duplicate incidents is methodologically undesirable but can hardly be excluded in principle. (3) An originally independent saying (v 28) of v 27 (e.g., Perrin, *Rediscovering,* 63–64; D. Lührmann, *Die Redaktion der Logienquelle,* WMANT 33 [Neukirchen, 1969] 33; Schurmann, *Gottes Reich,* 107–8). The unlikelihood of the sequence as a whole or v 28 in particular originating in the post-Easter communities is covered in 3b and 3c of text.

32. Cf. Fitzmyer, *Luke,* 2:922.

33. Sanders evades the particular issue of the distinctiveness of Jesus the exorcist by hypothesizing the likelihood that other first-century messianic prophets (e.g., Theudas and the Egyptian) would have "thought that God was at work in them and would bring in his kingdom through them" (*Jesus,* 138). But an appeal to an unattested possibility against an explicit testimony can hardly be given much weight.

(c) At the same time it would be hard to argue that the saying reflects the theology and concerns of the early churches. As we noted above, the early churches do not seem to have given much place or emphasis to exorcism—Christian exorcism being featured only twice in Acts and nowhere in the letters of the New Testament or even in the Fourth Gospel. Talk of the kingdom is similarly muted, and the most typical link between Spirit and kingdom seems to draw upon an established formulation in which the Spirit is seen as the earnest or guarantee of the still *future* kingdom yet to be inherited (Rom 8:14–17; 1 Cor 6:9–11; 15:44–50; Gal 4:29–30; 5:21–22; Eph 1:13–14; Tit 3:5–7; and cf. Acts 13:52 with 14:22).

In short, it is very hard to explain Mt 12:28/Lk 11:20 as originating either from the Jewish context of Jesus' ministry or from the theological concerns of the first Christians. Matthew 12:28/Luke 11:20 is one of relatively few sayings within the Jesus-tradition which comes strongly through the criterion of double dissimilarity—generally acknowledged to be overly stringent as a criterion for recognizing words of the historical Jesus.[34] The most obvious conclusion therefore is that the saying does indeed go back to Jesus, that Jesus was remembered as having attributed his prowess as an exorcist to the eschatological power of God, and thus that he saw his exorcisms as a manifestation of God's final reign already in operation.

Mt 12:28/Lk 11:20—
The Criterion of Coherence

A further factor in favor of tracing Mt 12:28/Lk 11:20 back to Jesus is the degree to which it coheres with other sayings within the Jesus-tradition.

(a) Mark 3:27/Luke 11:21–22 is a generalized proverbial saying which only gains its point by reference to a particular situation. Its reference in both Mark and Q is exorcism, and since the Mark and Q versions are so different they provide independent testimony on this point. We may take it then that this miniature parable was remembered from the first as a saying of Jesus about his exorcistic ministry.

---

34. Sanders makes some pertinent criticisms of this criterion (*Jesus*, 16–17) but also makes good use of it later (pp. 174, 252–53).

In this context the force of the proverb would be clear: the partial echo of Isa 49:24–26 (cf. Ps Sol 5:3) would suggest an eschatological significance; in reference to exorcism "the strong man" would readily be understood as Satan; the idea of the devil using a man as his "instrument" (σκεῦος) would cause no difficulty (T Naph 8:6; cf. Apoc Mos 16:5; 26:1; 31:4; Asc Isa 1:9; 2:1–4; 5:15). In particular, the saying would most likely evoke the Jewish expectation that Satan would be vanquished at the end of the age (Isa 24:21–22; 1 Enoch 10:4ff.; Jub 23:29; 1QS 4:18–19; T Mos 10:1; T Levi 18:12; T Jud 25:3; Rev 20:2–3).[35] In short, in this saying Jesus would almost certainly be understood to be claiming that his exorcisms constituted part of or evidence of the eschatological defeat of Satan. In other words, the point is the same as that in Mt 12:28/Lk 11:20: Mk 3:27/Lk 11:21–22 confirms that Jesus saw his exorcisms as manifestations of God's eschatological power already in operation. It is somewhat surprising then that Sanders at no point draws Mk 3:27/Lk 11:21–22 into the discussion of Mt 12:28/Lk 11:20 or considers it as possible evidence for the "present" emphasis in Jesus' talk of the kingdom.

(b) Of the other sayings material, Sanders designates Mt 11:5–6/Lk 7:22–23 as the most important. Here again his discussion focuses on the charges of circularity[36] and does not come to grips with the content of the saying or its context. Since I have discussed the passage in detail before, I may be permitted merely to summarize the chief points of that discussion.[37] The key to

35. Sanders narrows "the evidence usually cited" to T Mos 10:1 and T Levi 18 and thus is able to question whether we can speak of "a view common in Judaism" (*Jesus,* 134–35). But the range of evidence that I have cited in the text is proof enough that the eschatological demise of Satan was widely anticipated in Jewish expectation, whether expressed in terms of binding or in relation to a particular messianic figure.

36. Sanders, *Jesus,* 136–37.

37. Dunn, *Jesus,* 55–60. Sanders' one-sentence description of my discussion gives a misleading impression. My discussion showed how difficult it was to explain the question-answer sequence of Mt 11:2–6 on the presupposition that the account was a post-Easter construction. I concluded: "question and answer fit so neatly within the life-situation of Jesus and lack coherence if either or both were first prompted by a post-Easter situation, that the substance at least of the account must be regarded as historical. Jesus' words in vv 4–6 only really make

the exegesis of Mt 11:2–6/Lk 7:18–23 is to uncover the most satisfactory relation between the question of the Baptist, "Are you he who is to come . . . ?" and the answer of Jesus, "Go and tell John what you hear and see: the blind receive their sight and the lame walk . . . and the poor have good news preached to them." Why that question and answer? The key is provided most obviously by the recognition that Jesus' ministry did not fulfill the Baptist's prediction of what was about to happen (Mt 3:7–12/Lk 3:7–9, 16–17; cf. Mt 11:16–19/Lk 7:31–35; Mk 2:18–19). The unspoken promise behind the Baptist's query is based on the fact that Jesus had been making claims or acting in ways that did not match John's expectation and which seemed to call John's own message of eschatological judgment in question. The reply of Jesus in turn draws heavily on Isaiah's prophecies of the new age (Isa 29:18–19; 35:5–6; 61:1–2), which contain both promise of blessing and warning of judgment. But Jesus alludes only to the promised blessings. The answer to the Baptist in effect, then, is that the Baptist's expectation of judgment was inaccurate or lopsided. Jesus' ministry was marked rather by the realization of the promised blessings. Such a question and answer make best sense any time after the difference between John and Jesus became obvious and any time before the cross became a decisive factor in the Jesus-tradition, making necessary a more nuanced treatment of the themes of judgment and blessing (cf. e.g., Mk 2:19–20; 10:37–40). The corollary is obvious: Mt 22:5 is best explained as an expression of Jesus' enacted claim for the eschatological significance of his ministry, in other words, his claim that the benefits of God's final rule were already being enjoyed by those to whom he ministered. In short, the evidential value of Mt 11:5 for our present enquiry is not dependent on reading overtones of realized eschatology into it. These overtones are present in the Isaianic allusions; the saying makes excellent sense in its context; and it fits well with the sufficiently attested fact of a crucial difference between the Baptist and Jesus. The claim to coherence with Mt 12:28/Lk 11:20 cannot be dismissed as mere circularity.

(c) Space does not permit a more extensive analysis of other sayings in the Jesus-tradition that bear upon this issue. Suffice it

sense as an answer to such a question posed by the disciples of the Baptist" (p. 60).

to note that there are a number of such sayings whose *prima facie* sense coheres well with the implication that Jesus saw his ministry as a form of eschatological fulfillment of Isaiah's hopes—particularly Mt 9:37–38/Lk 10:2; Mt 11:11/Lk 7:28; Mt 11:12/Lk 16:16; Mt 12:41–42/Lk 11:31–32; Mt 13:16–17/Lk 10:23–24; Lk 17:20–21. Sanders is quite justified in pointing out that in themselves they are not explicit enough to sustain the claim that Jesus spoke of the kingdom as already present in his ministry.[38] However, read alongside the sayings already examined, they certainly provide clear enough evidence of a consistent emphasis of "realized eschatology" in the Jesus-tradition. With Lk 10:23–24 and 11:31–32 in particular it is surely highly dubious to argue that what the "prophets and kings desired to see" was simply someone announcing that the kingdom was at hand.[39] Which of Jesus' contemporaries would understand such language other than as a reference to the time of eschatological fulfillment of God's purposes for his people?

Moreover, the claim to be a medium of eschatological power embodied in Mt 12:28/Lk 11:20 fits well with other indications that Jesus understood his own ministry to be anointed and empowered by the Spirit. I am thinking particularly of the echoes of Isa 61:1 in Lk 6:20/Mt 5:3–4 and Mt 11:5/Lk 7:22 (cf. Lk 4:16–21), the implications of Mk 3:28–29/Q, and the clear indication that Jesus both spoke of himself and was widely understood in prophetic terms (particularly Mk 6:4 pars; 6:14–15 pars; 8:28 pars; 14:65 pars; Mt 21:11, 46; Lk 13:33; 24:19; Jn 6:14; 7:40, 52), with all that that would mean in terms of the eschatological restoration of the Spirit.[40]

In view of the diversity and range of these traditions, the most obvious conclusion is that the conviction of eschatological fulfillment in Jesus' ministry belongs to the bedrock of the tradition and that it has been retained despite its fitting awkwardly with the cross and even though the language was not always such as the first Christians would have chosen for themselves (as in Mt 11:12/Lk 16:16 and (c) above). The idea of God's

---

38. Sanders, *Jesus,* 148–49.
39. Ibid., 149.
40. See further Dunn, *Jesus,* 49–62, 82–84; also *Christology in the Making* (London: SCM, 1980) 137–41. On Mk 3:28–29/Q see above n. 21.

final rule already in operation through Jesus is a good deal more firmly rooted in the first Christians' earliest memories of Jesus than Sanders allows.

A Question of Method

I have to confess to having several misgivings over Sanders' methodology. Two have direct bearing on the present issue.

(a) At times Sanders gives the impression that he thinks he has successfully escaped the uncertainties inevitably bound up with the historical method. As noted above, he begins by parading his eight indisputable or almost indisputable facts.[41] The rationale of his subsequent analysis is that where these facts are illuminated by sayings which situate Jesus believably within first-century Judaism and which help explain the emergence of the Christian movement, the resultant conclusion can be elevated to a special status like that of the (almost) indisputable facts. Thus his conclusion contains a graded list of his findings, starting with five elements classed as "certain or virtually certain."[42] In the interim, however, his analysis has involved a considerable degree of interpretation, a good deal of which is very plausible and some of which is highly probable. But to what extent does the historical method enable us to treat the interpretation of a rather bare or generalized "fact" as itself "certain or virtually certain"? If, for example, "the (almost) indisputable fact" is that "Jesus engaged in controversy about the temple," is the more specific claim that Jesus expected a new (or at least restored) temple equally beyond question? I think not. The historical method is being asked at this point to deliver a greater degree of certainty than it is incapable of providing.[43]

---

41. See n. 11 above.
42. Sanders, *Jesus*, 326.
43. Cf. e.g., F. Hahn, "Problems of Historical Criticism," *Historical Investigation and New Testament Faith* (Philadelphia: Fortress, 1983): " . . . historical data cannot ultimately be illuminated by historical criticism, but in every case remain ambiguous, and their interpretation is therefore a matter of dispute. . . . The moment we pass beyond the description of facts and aim to give a substantive interpretation of the matters before us, we come up against the controversial nature of all historical occurrences" (p. 17).

(b) This overambitious use of the historical method also has its reverse side in *Jesus and Judaism*. Having made the claim that such a high level of probability is possible in some cases, Sanders evidently feels justified in applying rigorous tests to a saying like Mt 12:28/Lk 11:20: "in order to derive meaningful information about Jesus from such passages as Matt. 12:28 scholars must suppose . . . that they can reconstruct *precisely* what Jesus said and *precisely* what he meant by it. . . ."[44] But why such a rigorous demand? The issue focuses for Sanders in the verb φθάνειν, and of course we cannot be certain what was the precise expression which Jesus may have used. But the sense of φθάνειν is clear enough (to come, attain to, reach, arrive at),[45] so the note of realized eschatology is plain enough, whatever the precise form of an Aramaic underlay. Why we should need to reconstruct *precisely* what Jesus said and *precisely* what he meant is not clear. Elsewhere Sanders is content with the conclusion that the *general* expectation of a future coming of a heavenly figure probably goes back to Jesus.[46] And with regard to the crucial temple saying (Mk 14:58) he readily admits the unlikelihood of determining its original form with certainty.[47] No demand for precise reconstruction here! So quite why Mt 12:28

---

44. Sanders, *Jesus,* 138 (my italics).

45. *LSJ*, φθάνω; *TDNT* 9:88–91; Kümmel, *Promise,* 106–8; Lorenzmeier, 297–301. For the likely Aramaic underlay see G. Dalman, *The Words of Jesus* (Edinburgh: T. & T. Clark, 1902) 107. Sanders follows O'Neill in arguing that ἔφθασεν may mean "the coming was determined": not "the coming was accomplished" (Sanders, *Jesus,* 134, referring to O'Neill, *Messiah,* 16–18). The claim, however, is unsound. Of the passages referred to by O'Neill: Dan [Th] 4:24 refers to God's decree which Daniel is at that very moment in process of delivering to the king; T Ab (A) 1:5 is clearly a summary statement of the whole story which is about to unfold (cf. Dan [Th] 4:28); and 1 Thes 2:16 probably has in view God's eschatological wrath understood as already coming upon those resisting God's eschatological purpose unfolded in Jesus and in the mission to the Gentiles (cf. Rom 1:18; 11:8–9, 22; G. E. Ladd, *Jesus and the Kingdom* [London: SPCK, 1966] 138–39). The greater degree of ambiguity allowed by R. F. Berkey, "ἐγγίζειν, φθάνειν, and Realized Eschatology," *JBL* 82 (1963): 177–87, results primarily from his discussing the two verbs in relation to each other. On its own, the normal force of φθάνειν would indicate arrival or contact.

46. Sanders, *Jesus,* 144–45.

47. Ibid., 73.

should have to leap through the narrower hoop when Mk 14:58 is exempted is not at all clear. The historical method is being applied with insufficient consistency.

Rather we should recognize that the historical method does not by its very nature allow the sort of precision and certainty Sanders is looking for—neither with Jesus' talk of the kingdom's presence, nor with Jesus' expectation regarding the temple. Once the limitations of the historical method are thus recognized it should be clear that no such probability gap between Sanders' interpretation of Mk 14:58 and my interpretation of Mt 12:28/Lk 11:20 exists. If anything, I would be willing to claim that my interpretation of Mt 12:28/Lk 11:20 is more probable, but would be happy to settle for an equal rating on Sanders' scale of probability.

Conclusion

New Testament scholarship is in debt to Professor Sanders, not least because he forces us to rethink our presuppositions, method, and conclusions. But while I would wish to register agreement with a good deal of what he says in *Jesus and Judaism,* in this case I have to conclude that he has not followed the logic of his own method as well as he might.

As he would be the first to acknowledge, there is a danger of seeking a false consistency in such issues, of imposing on the evidence a consistency which is more of the interpreter's making than of the material's—nowhere more tempting than in the search for the resolution between the present and future emphases in the Jesus-tradition relating to the kingdom of God. But in this case Sanders seems to have allowed his initial reconstruction of Jesus' "restoration eschatology" and the admittedly less-than-adequate treatments of Mt 12:28/Lk 11:20 to push him to an unjustifiably minimal evaluation of that passage. Whereas, as we have now seen, its claim to serve as good evidence of something said by Jesus must be rated very highly.

In addition, Mt 12:28/Lk 11:20 contains more than a hint of how the tension between present and future in the kingdom material can be resolved: it was the experience (as Jesus understood it) of God's final rule already manifesting itself through him which probably convinced or reassured Jesus that the complete manifestation of that rule could not long be delayed.[48] To discount that evidence then is to narrow the reconstruction of the historical Jesus almost as much as does the misapplication of the criterion of double dissimilarity. Conversely, to appreciate its weight is to gain a further and deeper insight into the eschatology of Jesus, still tantalizing in its obscurities.[49]

It is a pleasure to dedicate this essay to one who from his earliest scholarship has made such distinguished contributions in this area—and who was kind enough not to fail my thesis eighteen years ago!

48. See further J. D. G. Dunn, "Spirit and Kingdom," *ExpTim* 82 (1970-71): 36-40. Lest the necessarily limited scope of this paper be misunderstood I should perhaps underscore my strongly held opinion that Jesus expected the full manifestation of God's rule (the end of history as we know it) imminently (Dunn, *Unity and Diversity in the New Testament* [London: SCM, 1977] 318-22). For this reason I welcome the main thrust of Sanders' ch 4: "Jesus looked for the imminent direct intervention of God in history . . ." (*Jesus,* 153). My disagreement is hardly at all with his "positive"; it is almost wholly directed against his "negative": that he limits the range of Jesus' talk of the kingdom unjustifiably and that he effectively excludes the note of eschatological fulfillment from Jesus' ministry.

49. I wish to record my appreciation to the other members of the postgraduate New Testament Seminar at Durham, whose theme for the first term of 1985-86 was Sanders' *Jesus and Judaism* and the issues raised by it. Our discussion and debate clarified and sharpened several important points. Prof. Sanders kindly joined in the discussion towards the end, and the outline of this paper was also discussed with him briefly, among several other matters arising from his book, in friendly debate at the University of Birmingham on November 9, 1985.

ESCHATOLOGY IN ACTS

4

F. F. Bruce
Professor Emeritus
University of Manchester

IT IS APPROPRIATE THAT a paper contributed as a small token of appreciation for Dr. Beasley-Murray's New Testament scholarship should deal with an aspect of biblical eschatology—a field of study which he has made specially his own. But it is contributed with two misgivings—one, that such a paper must appear pitifully amateurish when compared with Dr. Beasley-Murray's own contributions in this field, and the other, that "eschatology" may be an unsuitable term to cover some of the subject matter with which the paper will deal.

The term "eschatology" is no longer restricted in theological discussion to the traditional "last things"—death, judgment, heaven, and hell. The concepts of "realized," "proleptic," or "inaugurated" eschatology have brought the future into the present, and indeed into the past, so that one can sympathize with those voices that have recently urged that the very term "eschatology" should be expunged from our vocabulary because of its hopeless ambiguity, and replaced by others, each of which should express precisely one particular subject presently included in the vague area of "eschatology."[1]

Be that as it may, it is proposed to look at three topics in Acts which are involved in the winding up of the old order and the inauguration of the new.

1. See J. Carmignac, "Les Dangers de l'Eschatologie," *NTS* 17 (1970–71): 365–90.

The Restored Kingdom

A good place to start is with the apostles' question to the risen Lord: "Lord, will you at this time restore the kingdom to Israel?" (Acts 1:6). They did not receive a direct answer. It may be, however, that their question is answered indirectly, but adequately, at later stages in the narrative of Acts.

What did they understand by the restoration of the kingdom to Israel? Since, during his appearances to them in resurrection, the Lord is described as "speaking of the kingdom of God" (Acts 1:3), their question might be related to something he said to them. The kingdom of which he spoke during his ministry was the kingdom foretold in the book of Daniel, which the God of heaven was to set up in the latter days and which, superseding all previous world empires, was to endure for ever (Dan 2:44; 7:14). But the thought of the restoration of this kingdom *to Israel* does not match the language of Daniel. The kingdom in Daniel is to be given to "the (people of the) saints of the Most High" (Dan 7:18, 22, 27). In Luke's interpretation these are the disciples of Jesus, in accordance with a logion peculiar to the Third Gospel: "Fear not, little flock, for it is your Father's good pleasure to give you the kingdom" (Lk 12:32). One might argue that the little flock is the true Israel, but that does not seem to be the sense in which "Israel" is used in the apostles' question of Acts 1:6.

Another possibility is that they had in mind the restoration of the throne of David, with the national independence that such a restoration would involve. The restoration of the throne of David was not a theme of Jesus' recorded ministry. He was known to be a descendant of David (cf. Rom 1:3), and did not repudiate the designation "Son of David" when it was given to him (cf. Mk 10:47), but he did not appeal to any authority which his Davidic descent might be thought to give him; indeed, on the one occasion when he introduced the subject spontaneously, he played down its importance (Mk 12:35–37).

But the expectation of the Son of David was a live one in the circle into which he was born, if the canticles embedded in Luke's nativity narrative are to give us any guidance. The messianic hope which inspires them is not unlike that which inspired some of the Psalms of Solomon a generation or two earlier: in the face of the oppressive Roman ascendancy no deliverance can be expected apart from God's raising up the Son of David,

according to his ancient promise.[2] In this setting the angelic announcement about Mary's child had a clear meaning:

> The Lord God will give to him the throne of his father David, and
> he will reign over the house of Jacob for ever; and of his kingdom
> there will be no end (Lk 1:32f.).

The promise of Isa 9:6f. was recalled in these words; it was
about to be fulfilled.

To the same effect is Zechariah's outburst of praise to God, who

> has visited and redeemed his people,
> and has raised up a horn of salvation for us
> in the house of his servant David,
> as he spoke by the mouth of his holy prophets from of old,
> that we should be saved from our enemies,
> and from the hand of all who hate us (Lk 1:68–71).

To those "who were looking for the redemption of Jerusalem"
at that time such words were immediately intelligible; but in
the sense which they naturally placed upon these words they
were not realized. Yet Luke preserves these canticles in the introduction to his twofold history: what sense did he place upon
them? When he wrote, he knew that the Son of David had not
overthrown the Gentile oppressors or established national independence for Israel. Yet the promises on which those hopes
were based were not forgotten in the early church: their fulfillment was recognized and proclaimed. But it was a fulfillment
on a plane other than what formerly had been envisaged.

The promises made to the house of David were fulfilled in the
resurrection and exaltation of Jesus, the Son of David. This was a
recurrent note in the apostolic preaching, repeatedly recorded by
Luke. So Peter, on the day of Pentecost, is reported as declaring
that the oath sworn by God to David, "that he would set one
of his descendants upon his throne" (cf. Ps 132:11), has been fulfilled in Jesus, raised from the dead and now by God's right
hand exalted (Acts 2:29–36). The throne of David has been established eternally, because it has been established in the eternal realm, where the Son of David now reigns in perpetuity.

Similarly Paul, preaching one Sabbath in the synagogue of Pi-
sidian Antioch, surveyed the course of God's dealings with Israel
from the Exodus to the reign of David, and then moved straight
from David to Jesus: "Of this man's posterity God has brought to

2. Esp. PsSol 17:23–36.

Israel a Saviour, Jesus, as he promised" (Acts 13:23).[3] Samples of
the divine promises are quoted from the Psalter: "Thou art my
Son; today I have begotten thee" (Ps 2:7) and "Thou wilt not let
thy Holy One see corruption" (Ps 16:10)—a promise quoted
also by Peter in his Pentecost sermon and explained, as it is here
also, by the circumstances of Jesus' resurrection. These and related promises are summed up comprehensively as "the sure
mercies of David" (Isa 55:3)—the blessings graciously vowed to
David and now realized in the risen and enthroned Christ.

We need not trouble ourselves with arguments either that Peter's
speech is too Pauline or that Paul's speech is too Petrine: however
much of Peter or Paul finds expression in the speeches, their
Lukan authorship as they stand cannot be denied. We can see
how Luke understood the nativity canticles and also where he
found the answer to the apostles' question about the restoration of the kingdom to Israel. But, if the kingdom is restored by
the resurrection and enthronement of Christ, who constitutes
the Israel to whom it is restored? Are they those who acknowledge the sovereignty of Jesus as the Son of David? If they are,
Luke does not say so, and it would be unwise to put words into
his mouth. However, there is more to be said. David did not
reign over the house of Israel only, but extended his sway over
several neighboring nations. How is it with the Son of David?

Here great importance attaches to the interpretation of Amos
9:11f. in James' summing-up speech to the council of Jerusalem
(Acts 15:15–18). This oracle of hope, near the end of the book
of Amos, looks forward to the time when David's fallen "booth"
will be raised up again, when rulers of his house will not only
regain sovereignty over Israel but also "possess the remnant of
Edom and all the nations who are called by Yahweh's name."[4]

3. J. V. Doeve concludes that whoever composed this sermon
"must have had an excellent command of hermeneutics as practiced in
rabbinic Judaism" (*Jewish Hermeneutics in the Synoptic Gospels and
Acts* [Assen: Van Gorcum, 1954] 175f.); more specifically, J. W. Bowker
finds in this sermon a "proem homily" form ("Speeches in Acts: A
Study in Proem and Yelammedenu Form," *NTS* 14 [1967–68]: 101–10.

4. See J. Dupont, " 'Je rabâtirai la cabane de David qui est tombée
(Ac 15, 16 = Am 9, 11)," in *Glaube und Eschatologie: Festschrift für
W. G. Kümmel,* ed. E. Grässer and O. Merk (Tübingen: J. C. B. Mohr,
1985) 19–32. J. W. Bowker ("Speeches in Acts," 107–9) finds that
James's speech, with its appeal to scripture as confirming what has
been said or done already and what is about to be decided, "must be

Those nations (including Edom) were called by Yahweh's name in the sense that they were subjugated by David, a zealous worshiper of Yahweh, who accepted them as part of the heritage that Yahweh had bestowed on him.

It might seem far-fetched to see in this oracle a prediction and divine authorization of the church's Gentile mission, as James does in addressing the apostles and elders. But the Septuagint translators had already taken a long step in the direction of James' interpretation by spiritualizing the oracle. As they rendered it, it spoke no longer of military reconquest and subjugation, but of the turning of Israel's neighbors to seek the God of Israel, thanks to his people's witness to him and his mighty deeds. This is indeed a recurring theme in Isa 40–55: because Yahweh has reaffirmed his "steadfast, sure love for David" and made him "a witness to the peoples," therefore, he tells his restored people,

> you shall call nations that you know not,
> and nations that knew you not shall run to you,
> because of Yahweh your God,
> even the Holy One of Israel,
> for he has glorified you (Isa 55:3-5).

This, then, is the spirit which animates the Septuagint version of the Amos oracle. One clause only is materially changed: "that they may possess the remnant of Edom" has become "that the remnant of humanity may seek (me)." This change is partly due to scribal inadvertency and partly due to intentional reinterpretation.[5] The "remnant of humanity" that is to seek the Lord is identical with the sum total of the nations that are called by his name—in the Christian application, the sum total of Gentile believers in the gospel. The probability or improbability of James' quoting this Septuagint reading need not concern us here; what does concern us is that Luke, to whom the Gentile mission mattered greatly—was he not himself a Gentile by birth?—claims prophetic validation for it in these Old Testament words. Be-

---

understood as a genuine yelammedenu response'—so called because it is derived from a request for instruction: *yelammedenu rabbenu* ("let our teacher instruct us").

5. The change from *yîrešû* ("may possess") to *yidrešû* ("may seek") may have been a scribal slip, but the revocalization of *ĕdōm* as *ādām* ("mankind") is probably due to editorial policy.

cause Gentiles in such large numbers are now gladly yielding allegiance to the exalted Lord, great David's greater Son rules over many more Gentiles than David himself ever controlled. Not only in the resurrection and enthronement of Christ, but also in his acquiring so many believing Gentile subjects, the promises of the restoration of David's kingdom have received a much wider fulfillment than those to whom they were first made could have envisaged. Insofar as this perspective can be called eschatology, it is "realized" eschatology. But there is unrealized eschatology also to be recognized in Acts.

Judgment and Resurrection

It is part of the primitive kerygma that Jesus is the one appointed by God to conduct the end-time judgment of the world. This expectation appears in the early Pauline letters, in the sources of the Synoptic Gospels, in the Gospel of John and in both Petrine and Pauline speeches in Acts. In the house of Cornelius, Peter tells how the risen Christ commanded his disciples "to preach to the people, to testify that he is the one ordained by God to be judge of the living and the dead" (Acts 10:42). Before the court of the Areopagus in Athens, Paul concludes his discourse on the true knowledge of God with the announcement that, while God has overlooked people's ignorance of his nature thus far, he now commands universal repentance "because he has fixed a day on which he will judge the world in righteousness by a man whom he has appointed, and of this he has given assurance to all by raising him from the dead" (Acts 17:30, 31).

The proclamation of Jesus as the one through whom the final judgment is to be administered goes back to the identification of Jesus with Daniel's "one like a son of man" (Dan 7:13, 14), and this identification (if attention is paid to the variety of gospel strands which attest it) seems to have been made first by Jesus himself. Jesus may have chosen the self-designation "the Son of man" because it was not a term in current use, with a fixed meaning attached to it; he could therefore employ it without fear lest it might automatically convey to hearers a sense different from what he intended, and he could fill it with whatever meaning he chose. But on some occasions at least "the Son of man" on his lips meant "the (one like a) son of man" whom Daniel saw in his vision.[6] In Daniel's vision the one like

6. I have expanded this in "The Background to the Son of Man Say-

a son of man is assessor to the Ancient of Days in the final judgment, and receives universal and everlasting dominion from him. Jesus refers to this judicial role of the Son of man in a number of sayings—in Lk 12:8, for example, "every one who acknowledges me before men, the Son of man also will acknowledge before the angels of God,"[7] and quite notably in Jn 5:27, where the Father is said to have given the Son "authority to execute judgment, *because he is Son of man*."[8] But the most outstanding of all his references to the Son of man's judicial function is his answer to the high priest's question "Are you the Messiah?" "I am," was his reply; "and you will see the Son of man sitting at the right hand of Power, and coming with the clouds of heaven" (Mk 14:62).[9] His "I am" may be expanded to mean, "If you insist on framing your question in these terms, then I have no option but to say 'Yes'; but if I were to choose my own form of words, I should say that 'you will see the Son of man. . . .' " Here Daniel's vision, in which the "one like a son of man" is the Almighty's assessor in judgment, is combined with the oracle of Ps 110:1, where the Almighty invites an unnamed person (most probably the Davidic Messiah) to come and sit at his right hand. It was no doubt this claim to be God's assessor on the last day that elicited from the supreme court the unanimous verdict that Jesus was guilty of blasphemy. But, recognizing that God had vindicated his claim by raising him from the dead, Jesus' first disciples incorporated in their preaching from earliest days the affirmation that Jesus was the appointed judge of the living and the dead. In representing both Peter and Paul as making this affirmation, Luke represents them as reaffirming something that belonged to the apostolic preaching from the beginning. When Paul tells the Athenians that the pledge

---

ings" in *Christ the Lord: Studies in Christology presented to Donald Guthrie,* ed. H. H. Rawdon (Leicester: InterVarsity, 1982) 50–70.

7. This logion may underlie the use of "the Son of Man" in Acts 7:56 (the only NT occurrence of the expression outside the Gospels): Stephen has acknowledged Jesus before men, and now the Son of man stands up in the presence of God as his witness or advocate.

8. The exceptional absence of the article here is probably due to the fact that "Son of man" is the complement of the verb "is."

9. See D. R. Catchpole, "The Historicity of the Sanhedrin Trial," in *The Trial of Jesus—Cambridge Studies in Honor of C. F. D. Moule,* ed. E. Bammel (London: SCM Press, 1970) 47–65.

of Jesus' appointment as eschatological judge has been given by God in raising him from the dead, he voices no new insight but repeats an argument which impressed itself on the minds of the disciples from the very morrow of their Master's resurrection.

The resurrection of Christ is not only the pledge of his coming to judge the world; it is also the pledge of the resurrection of others. Paul presents this argument explicitly in 1 Corinthians 15, but he does so implicitly in his apologetic speeches in the closing chapters of Acts. When the commanding officer of the garrison in the Antonia fortress brought him before the Sanhedrin, Paul was not gratuitously throwing an apple of discord into the council chamber by declaring that he was on trial with regard to the hope of the resurrection of the dead (Acts 23:6). For Paul the hope of resurrection which he had learned to cherish as part of his pharisaic creed was confirmed by the resurrection of Christ, who appeared to him risen and exalted on the Damascus road, and called him to be his witness and apostle. Thenceforth the hope of resurrection, "the hope of Israel" (Acts 28:20), was bound up for Paul with the risen Christ. In preaching him, Paul was preaching the hope of Israel. "I stand here on trial," he said to the younger Agrippa, "for hope in the promise made by God to our fathers, to which our twelve tribes hope to attain" (Acts 26:6f.). It was not for the *general* hope of the resurrection that Paul was put on trial, but for his *specific* claim that the hope had already been fulfilled in one person, and by its fulfillment in him it was confirmed for all others. Paul's question, "Why is it thought incredible by any of you that God raises the dead?" (Acts 26:8), does not primarily relate to the future resurrection, as though it were a challenge addressed to Sadducees, but to a resurrection that has already taken place: "Why is it thought incredible by any of you," he means, "that God has raised Jesus his Son from the dead?"

Similarly, in his defense before Felix, Paul maintains his loyalty to his people's ancestral faith. Like his accusers, he says, he worships the God of their fathers, "believing everything laid down by the law or written in the prophets" and, more specifically, "having a hope in God which these themselves accept, that there will be a resurrection of both the just and the unjust" (Acts 24:24f.). The centrality of the resurrection hope for Paul comes to expression once more. More explicitly here than in any of the Pauline letters comes an assertion that the unjust as well as the just will be raised; this accords with the usual interpretation of Dan 12:2[10] and with the dominical affirmation of Jn 5:28f.

The resurrection hope of Israel, then, has been realized already in God's raising Christ from the dead; it remains thus far unrealized for others, but its realizing in the raising of Christ is the guarantee of its coming fulfillment for others. Paul's message of a risen Lord should therefore be welcomed by Israelites; it is (if only they knew it) the confirmation of God's promises to his people and of the hope which they base on his promises.

"Whom Heaven Must Receive Until . . ."

In the record of the healing of the lame man in the temple precincts, Peter seizes the opportunity provided by the crowd that gathered to see the amazing cure that had been effected, assuring it that Jesus, through whose name that man had been cured, was manifestly alive and powerful. God has raised him up and glorified him, thus reversing the rejection and death sentence so unjustly meted out to him.

> Repent therefore, and turn again, that your sins may be blotted out, that times of refreshing may come from the presence of the Lord, and that he may send you the Christ appointed for you, Jesus, whom heaven must receive until the time for establishing all that God spoke by the mouth of his holy prophets from of old (Acts 3:19–21).

The reference to "all that God spoke by the mouth of his holy prophets" is then illustrated by the quotation of Moses' words about the prophet like himself whom God would raise up (Dt 18:15, 19). But the words of Acts 3:19–21 themselves do not express a Prophet Christology anymore than they express a Servant Christology in line with the quotation from Isa 52:13 at

---

10. B. J. Alfrink, "L'idée de Resurrection d'après Dan. XII, 1.2," in *Studia Biblica et Orientalia* I, Analecta Biblica 10 (Rome: Pontifical Biblical Institute, 1959) 221–37, following Sa'adya Ga'on, interprets Dan 12:2b as meaning: "these (who are written in the book) will awake to everlasting life, but those (the others) will be left to shame and everlasting contempt." A similar distinction is made by S. P. Tregelles, *Remarks on the Prophetic Visions in the Book of Daniel* [London: S. Bagster, 1883] 165–70), who sees the first-named category as rising in the first resurrection, while the rest are left in the dust of the earth "until the thousand years were ended" (Rev 20:5).

the beginning of Peter's address to the crowd.[11] They express a quite distinctive Christology, and even if it should not be described as "the most primitive christology of all," as J. A. T. Robinson suggested,[12] the eschatology which they also express has a strong claim to be described as "the most primitive eschatology of all."

The members of the crowd, addressed as "men of Israel," are called upon to repent and so have their sins blotted out. In the context, their repentance involves a reappraisal of Jesus, in accordance with God's promulgated appraisal of him. If they repent, God will send them "times of refreshing." According to Eduard Schweizer, these "times of refreshing" are to be understood as "the definitive age of salvation," which God will send speedily if the hearers (and their fellow Israelites) repent.[13] To C. K. Barrett's mind, however, the expression "times of refreshing" suggests rather "moments of relief during the time men spend in waiting for that blessed day."[14] In any case, the "blessed day" will not be long delayed; its advent will be speeded by Israel's acceptance of Jesus as the one whom God has sent.

The essential features of this primitive expectation seem to have been inherited by Paul with other elements of Christian belief that he received on the morrow of his conversion, and they survive in his mature eschatological thinking, albeit modified by the new perspective which was his as apostle to the Gentiles. To Paul the parousia of Christ is the sequel to the salvation of Israel, if indeed the two events do not take place simultaneously (Rom 11:15, 26f.). Only, for Paul the salvation of Israel must follow the ingathering of the Gentiles; his own ministry in the Gentile world would be the indirect means of stimulating Israel's change of heart. At this earlier stage, however, the mission to the Gentiles is not in view; the overflow of Israel's blessing to Gentiles is at best hinted at in Peter's citation of the promise that in Abraham's posterity "all the families of the earth"

11. Acts 3:13a.

12. J. A. T. Robinson, "The Most Primitive Christology of All?" in *Twelve New Testament Studies* (London: SCM Press, 1962) 139–53.

13. E. Schweizer, *TDNT* 9:664, s.v. ἀναψύχω.

14. C. K. Barrett, "Faith and Eschatology in Acts 3," in *Glaube und Eschatologie,* 12.

would be blessed (Acts 3:25). But it is to Israel first that the blessing is sent.

The result of Israel's repentance, then, will be God's sending of Jesus as its appointed Messiah (Acts 3:20). It has been argued, indeed, that Jesus is here envisaged as being still Messiah designate; his installation as Messiah regnant awaits his appearance from heaven.[15] But there is nothing in the verb rendered "appointed" to suggest designation as distinct from full investiture; Jesus is already Messiah. In this regard the perspective of Peter's present temple speech is no different from that of his speech on the day of Pentecost, where it is by Jesus' resurrection and exaltation that God has made him "both Lord and Christ" (Acts 2:36).

But at present this Messiah is in heaven and he must remain there until the time comes for the fulfillment of all that God has spoken through his prophets (Acts 3:21).[16] The word ἀποκατάστασις, here translated "fulfillment" or "establishment," may also mean "restoration," "restitution," or "renewal"—the verb from which it is derived is the verb used in the apostles' question in Acts 1:6 about "restoring" the kingdom to Israel; although, if "restoration" is the meaning here, much more than the restoration of the kingdom to Israel is involved. A more relevant instance of this sense of ἀποκατάστασις, or rather of the corresponding verb, is in Mk 9:12 par Mt 17:11, where Elijah is expected to come and "restore all things" (in Mal 4:5 it is the restoration or reconciliation of the hearts of parents to children and vice versa that he is to effect). Otto Bauernfeind thought that at an earlier stage in the tradition Acts 3:20f. referred to *Elijah's* return from heaven, and that the original form of words has been adapted to the Christian expectation of Jesus' return. He reckoned it probable that the Elijah expectation was cherished among the disciples of John the Baptist.[17] More gen-

---

15. J. A. T. Robinson, "The Most Primitive Christology?" 144.

16. This interval corresponds to "the days of the Messiah" in rabbinical expectation—only, the Messiah does not spend those days on earth but in heaven.

17. O. Bauernfeind, *Die Apostelgeschichte* (Leipzig: A. Deichert, 1939) 66–68; "Tradition und Komposition in dem Apokatastasisspruch Apostelgeschichte 3, 20f.," in *Abraham unser Vater . . . Festschrift für Otto Michel,* ed. O. Betz, M. Hengel, and P. Schmidt (Leiden: Brill, 1963) 13–23.

erally the restoration or renewal of all things in the sense of all creation at the messianic advent is foretold in Rom 8:18–23 (cf. 4 Ezra 7:75; 13:26–29; 1 Enoch 45:5; 51:4, etc.); and one may think of the new world or "regeneration" of Mt 19:28.

There is thus no lack of parallels for ἀποκατάστασις, in the sense of restoration, and further instances could be adduced from Hellenistic inscriptions and papyri. Even so, in the context of Acts 3:19–21 the alternative meaning "fulfillment" or "establishment" makes good sense, in reference to the fulfillment of all Old Testament prophecy, culminating in the establishment of God's order on earth. This meaning, also attested in inscriptions and papyri, is borne by the related verb several times in the Septuagint, and seems to be better suited to the present context than the meaning "restoration."

The fulfillment of all the prophecies, then, coincides with Jesus' reappearance from heaven, and his reappearance can be expedited by Israel's repentance. This is not Luke's eschatology; but it should be recognized as the faithful reproduction of an early phase of Jewish-Christian eschatology. Luke's own eschatology has little room for the repentance of Israel. Although he does not say so explicitly, it would be in keeping with his general outlook if the consummation of all things coincided with the completion of the Gentile mission. Unlike Paul, he says nothing of the completion of the Gentile mission being the occasion for Israel's ultimate returning to the Lord. In Luke's eyes, from Jerusalem to Rome the Gentile mission is the result of Israel's repudiation of the gospel, and when at the end of the story Paul is heard saying to the representatives of the Roman Jews, "this salvation of God has been sent to the Gentiles; *they* will listen" (Acts 28:28), there is a definitive note about the words which holds out no hope of a future return to gospel faith on the part of Israel. With the gospel firmly planted at the heart of the Roman Empire, the future lies with the Gentile mission. When Paul disappears from the scene, the Gentile mission will go on. How long it may be before it is completed Luke does not know, but plainly he does not expect its completion to take place the day after tomorrow. Whether or not he regards the current phase of history as "the period of the church," it is the age of gospel expansion and is likely to go on for a considerable time to come. There is nothing in Acts to throw light on the dominical logion about "the times of the Gentiles" in Lk 21:24 (there is no obvious connection between that period and the age of Gentile evangelization), nor is any hint given in Acts about what will happen when those "times" are "fulfilled."[18]

Luke's perspective could probably be summed up in the logion of Mark 13:10: "the gospel must first be preached to all the nations." True, this logion is not reproduced in Luke's edition of the Olivet discourse; but that may be because Luke tends to reserve some material found in his gospel sources for inclusion in his second volume, if the subject is more appropriate to the theme of the second volume. The second volume tells how the gospel began to be preached to all the nations. Luke, it is suggested, reckoned that when this process had been completed, then the consummation would come.

As these words are written, I reflect that it is exactly forty-five years ago that I first met George Beasley-Murray. At that time he had recently taken his first degree, and was about to embark on a program of research—in the first instance, on our Lord's Olivet discourse (Mark 13). His program of research is still being carried on—not only in eschatology and the kingdom of God but in other areas of Christian concern. His contributions to scholarship have put all of us who have a care for biblical studies greatly in his debt. May that debt go on increasing! He will be none the poorer, but we shall be much the richer. *In multos annos!*

18. *Die Mitte der Zeit* (Tübingen: J. C. B. Mohr, 1957) is the original title of the work by Hans Conzelmann known in its English translation as *The Theology of St. Luke* (New York: Harper/London: Faber, 1960).

THE GENTILE MISSION AS AN ESCHATOLOGICAL PHENOMENON

5

C. K. Barrett
Professor of Divinity, Emeritus
University of Durham

THAT THE CHRISTIAN MISSION is directed to the whole world is today a proposition taken for granted without argument. It was not always so, and the early Christian mission to Gentiles constitutes a problem in more senses than one. That it was a problem to the first-century church is attested by the clearest firsthand evidence. There were those who would prevent Paul from speaking to the Gentiles that they might be saved (1 Thes 2:16). These were Jews, apparently not Christians. But there were also Christians who would consent to the inclusion of Gentiles among the people of God only on terms that would have excluded many: they wished all converts to be circumcised (Gal 6:12). This leads to the somewhat less direct evidence of Acts, where the same demand is made: "Unless you are circumcised in accordance with the custom of Moses you cannot be saved . . . It is necessary to circumcise them [Gentile converts] and order them to keep the law of Moses" (Acts 15:1, 5). Already Peter's approach to Cornelius had attracted criticism (11:3), and it was only by a vision that he had himself been persuaded that God had no favorites and that he must call no one profane or unclean (10:28, 34). It was by no means clear to the earliest Christians (for we have no reason to question the sincerity of those who opposed the movement into the Gentile world) that Christian missionaries should be free to present the gospel to those who were Jews neither by birth nor by proselytization. Hence a second sense in which the Gentile mission constitutes a problem: it is a problem to the historian of Christian thought and action, who is bound to ask why so many of the first Christians adopted this limiting attitude; what arguments and what events convinced them, or a majority of them, to abandon it; and how, in this controversial situation, the mission proceeded.

Like many problems and controversies, this, though it evoked strong feeling and sharp dispute, proved in the end to be creative. It would suffice to refer to Paul, whose understanding of law, faith, and grace was sharpened by the debate in which he found himself involved; beyond Paul lies the unquestioned universal scope of Christian evangelism which ultimately emerged—threatened though it regrettably was in the later stages by the opposite danger of neglecting, despising, and even hating the Jews. The missionary problem moreover interacted with another of the major problems of the early years, that of eschatology. The reconstruction of the earliest Christian outlook upon the future affords plenty of room for controversy and debate (to which Dr. Beasley-Murray has made a distinguished contribution), but few are likely to disagree with the moderate proposition that in the first years of the church there were at least some, perhaps many, who believed that the time before the end was too short to admit any extension of the mission beyond the confines of Israel. Such an extension might or might not be desirable, permitted, or illicit; it was simply impossible. It was a natural inference that what God's plans did not permit he cannot have desired. How widespread this view was, and whether it went back to Jesus, are questions that will be briefly touched upon below; if it existed at all, that is sufficient to demonstrate the association that has been made between the problem of the Gentile mission and the problem of eschatology, and goes some way towards vindicating the description of the Gentile mission as an eschatological phenomenon.

What follows is anything but a full discussion of the question in what sense the Gentile mission may be spoken of as an eschatological phenomenon. Its main intention is to consider the bearing on the matter of some passages in Acts, but it is necessary first to glance briefly at the teaching of Jesus and Paul—briefly, because the essential points are not unfamiliar.

Jesus

Did Jesus himself carry out, plan, or desire a mission to the non-Jewish world? The correct answer to this question has, in my opinion, been given by Joachim Jeremias in *Jesus' Promise to the Nations.* The evidence contained in the Gospels appears to lead to a contradiction.

> We have found, on the one hand, that Jesus limited his activity to Israel, and imposed the same limitation upon his disciples. On the other hand, it has been established that Jesus expressly promised the Gentiles a share in the Kingdom of God, and even warned his Jewish hearers that their own place might be taken by the Gentiles.[1]

The contradiction is resolved by the recognition that "the gathering in of the Gentiles occurs in the hour of the final judgement."[2] Jesus believed that the Gentiles would be drawn (as the Old Testament had foretold[3]) at the end of time to the Mount of God. It was God's intention that they should eventually share his kingdom with the Jews, but this would not happen as the result of a mission conducted in the course of history. It would be in the strictest sense a matter of eschatology, not of "realized eschatology" but of that ultimate future which, however near, lies beyond the present span of time.

Jeremias recognizes that Mark and the other synoptic evangelists do contemplate a mission in historical terms; this was inevitable since they lived in the midst of the mission; but where they allow this to appear they are reinterpreting sayings of Jesus which may originally have borne a different meaning. The two most important passages are Mk 13:10 and 14:9. Each of these must be interpreted in terms of the angelic proclamation of good news described in Rev 14:6f., "where, in the hour of final fulfillment, an angelic voice proclaims 'the everlasting gospel of triumph.' "[4] This belongs to the last day, when the Gentiles are included in God's people at God's own instance. This is Jesus' view, modified by the Gospel editors, who knew that a historical mission was in fact taking place. Whether Jeremias had rightly interpreted the Marcan passages is a fair question,

---

1. J. Jeremias, *Jesus' Promise to the Nations,* (Philadelphia: Fortress, 1983), 55.
2. Ibid., 56.
3. Isa 2:2–4; Mic 4:1–3.
4. Jeremias, *Promise,* 22.

and one that can be properly treated only in the context of a general discussion of the eschatology of Jesus and of the evangelists. Of the teaching of Jesus it would be hard to affirm anything with complete conviction beyond the fact that he believed that his ministry would culminate in an eschatological crisis of rejection by the people and vindication by God. The vindication was expressed in various ways which appear to be alternative images rather than sequential stages. The image of resurrection was used; the image of an appearance with the clouds of heaven was used also. The two never appear in the same prediction in such a way as to suggest that there would be an interval between them.

If it is indeed true that Jesus (whatever he may himself have thought inwardly) gave no explicit instruction about such an interval, two things, otherwise difficult to explain, become clear. In the first place, it is easy to see why there was much hesitation and not a little dispute about the inauguration of a mission to the Gentiles. If Jesus had in fact given orders that such a mission should take place in the interval between his resurrection and his return, his followers could hardly have disputed whether it was right to undertake it. If, on the other hand, resurrection happened and the expected parousia did not, the disciples must have asked themselves in some bewilderment what they were expected to do—wait another week or two in Jerusalem, doing nothing? They can hardly be blamed if they found a worldwide mission not immediately obvious. In the second place, the diversity of attempts to fill the gap is accounted for. There are passages, such as Mk 13:10 and 14:9, which speak fairly plainly of a mission to Gentiles, and Mk 7:19 claims that at least the laws regarding clean and unclean foods are abrogated. On the other hand, Mt 10:5, 6, 23 order missionaries to confine their work to Israel; they must not approach Gentiles. Matthew does not reproduce Mk 7:19, and Mt 5:17 requires the observance of even the least commandments. Matthew himself has reached a point at which variety can be accommodated. Along with the passages cited he gives (28:19) the commission to make disciples of πάντα τὰ ἔθνη ("all the nations") and appears to understand the restrictive commands as applying to the time of the ministry of Jesus, the universal commission to the post-resurrection interval.

The Gentile mission thus appears as a piece of "realized eschatology" belonging to the period between resurrection and parousia.

Paul

Paul could describe himself as ἐθνῶν ἀπόστολος ("an apostle of the Gentiles," Rom 11:13), and it seems that he had to defend himself against the charge of neglecting his own people. His protestations in Rom 9:2f. and 10:1 are so strong that they are best understood as a reply to charges that had hurt his image. He was in truth willing to exchange Christ's blessing for his curse if that would benefit his fellow Jews. It was by agreement that he concentrated his mission on the Gentile world; at his meeting in Jerusalem with James, Cephas, and John, he and Barnabas had undertaken to "go to the Gentiles" leaving the Jewish mission field to the Jerusalem apostles (Gal 2:9). Exactly how this agreement was understood and how it was carried out cannot be discussed here; Paul certainly did not take it to mean that he might never offer the gospel to Jews or have Jews in his churches. He did, however, both practise and defend the mission to Gentiles, whom he received into the church without any demand that they should become Jews on the way.

Paul answered the charge that he was a renegade, neglecting his own people in the interests of others, not only with vehement assertion of his devotion to his kinsmen after the flesh but also by a reassessment of the eschatological situation. Those who took the line suggested by Mt 10:23 and applied it to the time after the resurrection must have argued, There is no time for a mission to the Gentiles. It will be hard enough to cover the cities of Israel before the coming of the Son of man; we must concentrate first on our fellow Jews. If God wishes to have some Gentiles among his chosen people he can bring them to Zion at the last day. They may well have continued, To go to the Gentiles at the same time as to the Jews will not only cost time and effort that we cannot afford; it will also make the conversion of Israel more difficult because Jews will not wish to be associated with Gentiles, probably of low ethical achievement and certainly unclean by the standards and requirements of the law. This argument Paul answered by a special divine "revelation," a μυστήριον (Rom 11:25). At least a partial failure of the mission to Israel is assumed; this is certainly in accordance with fact. It must already in the 50s have been clear that only a minority of Jews were accepting Jesus as Messiah. The answer to this was not to go on battering on a closed door but to turn, as Paul had done, to the Gentiles. It was God's intention not to draw in the Gentiles as a sort of afterthought, with the intention of filling up the vacant places left by recalcitrant Jews, but to incorporate them first. First the πλήρωμα τῶν ἐθνῶν ("fulness of the Gentiles," 11:25), then Israel—πᾶς 'Ισραὴλ σωθήσεται ("all Israel will be saved," 11:26). The process is given a psychological explanation in 11:14: Paul will pursue his Gentile mission with the utmost vigor: εἴ πως παραζηλώσω μου τὴν σάρκα καὶ σώσω τινὰς ἐξ αὐτῶν. To see Gentiles included and themselves rejected will provoke the Jews to jealousy, and they will turn to claim their own. Later in the chapter Paul gives a theological explanation. This has two points. If God calls individuals (as he has certainly called Israel) he does not stop calling them even when he is rebuffed (11:28, 29). Israel is therefore not to be written off. But also: the only basis on which God deals with humanity is mercy. There is no person, Jew or Gentile, who can deserve salvation; as long as they suppose that they can deserve it they will not have it. Only out of a context of recognized unbelief and disobedience will people accept God's mercy. The Gentiles were, and knew that they were, already in this context. Hence the success of Paul's mission to them; they knew that they had no righteousness of their own and were therefore prepared to accept the righteousness offered them by the mercy of God in Christ. The Jews were seeking (according to Rom 10:3) to establish their own righteousness; only when their disobedience, proved by their rejection of the Messiah, was demonstrated would they recognize that they too had no hope except in the mercy of their own merciful God. Israel's salvation would come about only by the removal of sin (11:27, quoting Isa 59:21).

Paul's revelation[5] is put in an eschatological setting. Salvation is regularly for Paul a future event (cf. e.g., Rom 13:11). Here, however, the future is represented as already invading the present. The Jews have *now* become disobedient and unbelieving (νῦν ἠπείθησαν), that they may *now* be dealt with in mercy

5. Cf. the use of μυστήριον in an apocalyptic setting of 1 Cor 15:51.

(νῦν ἐλεηθῶσιν, 11:31). It is in the light of God's final action, not only of Paul's evangelistic mission, that πλήρωμα ("fulness") and πᾶς ("all") must be understood.

Acts

Whether the "delay of the parousia" played a major part in the motivation of Acts is a disputed question which need not be considered here. What is clear beyond dispute is that had there been no interval between resurrection and parousia there would have been no Christian history for Luke or anyone else to record. It is equally clear that the mission to the Gentiles was one of Luke's keenest interests. It forms the backbone of his book. If Philip's mission to the Samaritans and to an Ethiopian, the founding by Peter of an at least partly Gentile church in Caesarea, and the founding of a similar church in Antioch are removed from the first twelve chapters, little is left; and the rest of Acts (13–28) is an account of the work of the great Gentile missionary Paul, punctuated only by an account of the council, which both defended and regulated his work. Another observation regarding Acts is that though Luke has by no means abandoned futurist eschatology, he has it firmly under control so that it has no problems for him. In the opening chapter it is made clear that Jesus who ascends into heaven with a cloud will come in the same way (1:11); the story of the church and its mission will be terminated by the return of Christ. God knows when this will happen; he has established times and seasons by his own authority (1:7), and he has set a day when he will judge the world in righteousness (17:31). But no one else knows when the end will be. He leaves it to his Christians to get on with the job he has appointed for them; and this for Luke means the evangelization of both Jews and Gentiles, a process which is located within what remains of the present age. The sun has not yet been turned into darkness nor the moon into blood; the present is the time of vision and prophecy, in which everyone who invokes the Lord's name will be saved (Acts 2:17–21).

This was Luke's own view. The mission is not so much a matter of "realized eschatology" as of a substitute for an eschatology that has been deferred. But Luke, open to criticism though his historical work is, did not write the story of the church simply out of his own imagination but on the basis of traditions—some written, some oral, some trustworthy, others clearly fallible—helped out by his own reconstruction. It is for us to look among these traditions to detect, if we can, traces of earlier eschatological thought. They are not many; Luke absorbed and digested his material.

The interesting (and to me unexpected) result of this inquiry is that Luke shows here and there traces of the view that we have seen to be opposed to the conviction that Paul had reached by the time he wrote Romans 9–11. Acts confirms the view that there were those who held that the prime obligation of Christians before the End was to win the Jews.

We can lay little stress on the sequence Jerusalem, Judaea, Samaria, the end of the earth (1:8); this was probably Luke's own programme for his work (cf. Lk 24:47) and in any case does little more than express an inevitable geographical expansion from the center.

The appointment of a twelfth witness in the place of Judas Iscariot has been well explained by K. H. Rengstorf.[6] The Twelve were to be the eschatological judges of Israel (Mt 19:28; Lk 22:30); the appointment of Matthias meant that notwithstanding the crucifixion the disciples were not abandoning their responsibility for and to Israel. The mission to the Jews must be reestablished before anything else was done, and it must be done in view of what was to happen at the παλιγγενεσία (the word is Matthew's but the sense of it is also in Luke 22).

The evidence of Acts 2 is difficult to handle and to harmonize. The list of names in 2:9–11 is so oddly assorted and arranged that one hesitates to draw the conclusion[7] that it represents the gathering of the Gentiles to Mount Zion, thus anticipating the End.[8] Did not Luke think that all concerned were Jews or proselytes? This seems to be the view expressed in the speech; note the reference to πᾶς οἶκος Ἰσραὴλ in v 36 ("all the house of Israel"). This in turn suggests that v 39 means "to you Pal-

---

6. K. H. Rengstorf, "Die Zuwahl des Matthias," *Studia Theologica* 15 (1962): 35–67; idem, "The Election of Matthias," *Current Issues in New Testament Interpretation: Essays in Honor of Otto Piper,* ed. W. Klassen and G. F. Snyder (New York: Harper, 1962) 178–92, 293–96.

7. Notwithstanding H. J. Cadbury's view that Gentiles were intended.

8. See above, pp. 69ff.

estinian Jews and to your distant brethren in the Diaspora." It does, however, seem probable that Luke wished to suggest by his list of names and the reference to οἱ εἰς μακράν ("those from afar") that gospel and church were from the beginning at least potentially universal.

It is only towards the close of the speech in ch 3 that Peter begins to envisage the world outside Judaism and then in such a way as to suggest that the Gentiles take a second place. The word πρῶτον ("first," v 26) is explicit, and it interprets the promise to Abraham quoted in v 25: ἐν τῷ σπέρματί σου ἐνευλογηθήσονται πᾶσαι αἱ πατριαὶ τῆς γῆς. Instructed by Paul in Gal 3:16 we are accustomed to take the *seed of Abraham* as a - reference to Christ, but in v 25a *you*, the Jewish hearers of Peter's speech, have been described as οἱ υἱοὶ τῶν προφητῶν καὶ τῆς διαθήκης ἧς διέθετο ὁ θεὸς πρὸς τοὺς πατέρας ὑμῶν. *They* are the seed of Abraham; in *them*, once they have come to accept Jesus as the Messiah and to find in him the forgiveness of their sins, the Gentile families will be blessed. That is, the Gentiles will indeed be accepted, but in a second stage of the mission.

For several reasons which are not to be discussed here it would be unwise to build a great deal on Acts 8:14 and 11:22, but if these verses are taken as they stand they indicate suspicion regarding any advance towards the Gentiles.

The most interesting piece of evidence is the quotation from Amos 9:11f., attributed in Acts 15:16–18 to James. This has recently been discussed afresh by J. Dupont,[9] whose article contains a wealth of bibliographical references[10] which it is unnecessary to repeat here. He concludes,

If it can be assumed that Luke has some consistency in his views, then when in Acts 15:16 he writes on the issue of the restoration of

9. J. Dupont, " 'Je rabâtirai la cabane de David qui est tombée' Ac 15,16 = Am 9,11," in *Glaube und Eschatologie: Festschrift für W. G. Kümmel,* ed. E. Grässer and O. Merk (Tübingen: J. C. B. Mohr, 1985) 19–32.

10. One could add now the commentary Ökemenischer Tashenbuch-Kommentar zum Neuen Testament, 5/1 and 5/2, 1981 and 1985, by A. Weiser; and a further article by J. Jervell, "Die Mitte der Schrift," *Die Mitte des Neuen Testaments: Festschrift für Eduard Schweizer,* ed. U. Luz and H. Weder (Göttingen: Vandenhoeck & Ruprecht, 1983) 79–96 published in English as "The Center of Scripture" in J. Jervell, *The Unknown Paul* (Minneapolis: Augsburg, 1984) 122–37, 179–83.

the tabernacle of David, presenting it as the point of departure for the offering of salvation to the Gentiles, one should not consider this simply (*simplement*) as a restoration of Israel that will be achieved in the Judaeo-Christian community. The "tabernacle" of David is none other than the "house" of David seen in the pathetic state in which it found itself at the time of the division of the monarchy. It must not be confused with the "house of Israel" (Acts 2:36; 7:42). This house of David was rebuilt and the throne of David reerected at the moment in which God raised Jesus to be seated at his right hand (2:34). From the perspective of Luke, the "universal" nature of Christian mission is rooted directly in the mystery of Easter.[11]

With this proposition I should agree provided I were allowed to lay great stress, greater stress, I suspect, than Père Dupont would himself allow, on the word *simplement*. It is true that the very name David points in a messianic direction, and it is also true that Christian universalism is rooted in the "mystère de Pâques," though how far this entered into "l'optique de Luc" is another question. Père Dupont's view is supported by his review of Jewish interpretation of Amos 9:11f.,[12] but he does not, I think, allow sufficient weight to the context in which the quotation appears, and, in particular, to the somewhat obscure argument conducted by James. This leads to a conclusion that James (no doubt we should say, Luke) cannot have found easy to state. Acts 15:19, 20 could almost be paraphrased, I give my judgement that we should not trouble (παρενοχλεῖν) Gentiles who are turning to God—at least, that we should not trouble them too much. We will not ask them to observe the whole law, but we will ask for certain limited observances. This is followed by the notoriously obscure v 21, which gives a ground (γάρ) for the "decree," but does not make clear whether it is defending it against the charge that it asks too much or the charge that it asks too little. There are in fact two interests to be served, those of the Jewish-Christian and those of the Gentile-Christian communities. With this balance the quotation from Amos is well chosen to agree, and though Père Dupont calls it a "curieuse consideration" (p. 31, n. 41), J. Jervell's argument that as v 17 has in mind the Gentile church so v 16 will refer to the Jewish church is by no means without weight. His point is given in the

11. Dupont, "Je rebâtirai la cabane de David," 31f.
12. Dupont refers to Dan 11:14; CD 7:14–19; 4Q 174 1:10–13; b. Sanhedrin 96b.

words, "Die Bekehrung der Heiden ist die Erfüllung der Verheissungen an Israel . . . Dies stimmt mit dem jüdischen Gedankengang überein, nachdem die Heiden in der Endzeit sich dem wiederaufgerichteten Israel anschliessen werden."[13]

It would be natural to infer from this that Christians must take as their priority the establishing of a renewed Jewish people, united in the acceptance of the Messiah Jesus. Without this, to what could Gentile converts attach themselves? The practical consequence was that potential Jewish converts must not be frightened off by too strong a measure of Gentile freedom. This attitude and programme correspond with Paul's theological statement, "to the Jew first and also to the Greek,"[14] but also with that whose existence was inferred from Paul's energetic reply in Romans 9–11.[15]

Both attitudes, Paul's and the other, are intelligible, especially if it is true that Jesus left his followers with no instructions about the way they should conduct themselves in the interval between resurrection and parousia. That both existed helps to make intelligible the conflicts that lie under the surface of the narrative of Acts, and on the surface of the Pauline letters. Paul shows a greater readiness to respond to the historical circumstances in which the eschatology of the Gospels and of the gospel is to be worked out, and a greater readiness to look to the future: it is neither circumcision nor uncircumcision that counts, but a new act of creation (Gal 6:15).

13. J. Jervell, "Das gespaltene Israel und die Heidenvolker," *Studia Theologica* 19 (1965): 68–96; quotation from 80f. ET: "The conversion of the Gentiles is the fulfillment of the promises to Israel. . . . This corresponds with Jewish thinking, according to which in the endtime the Gentiles will be joined with reestablished Israel."

14. Rom 1:16; 2–9, 10. Can these have been a concession to opponents? Cf. also the allegory of the olive tree, Rom 11:17–24.

15. See above, pp. 69–71. See also ch. 6 in this volume.

THE FUTURE OF ISRAEL: REFLECTIONS ON ROMANS 9-11

6

*Günter Wagner
Professor of New Testament
Baptist Theological Seminary*

IN OUR ATTEMPT TO UNDERSTAND what Paul has to say in Romans 9-11 about the future of Israel, we shall proceed by *first* sketching the development of thought in these three chapters; *second,* we shall offer some suggestions for the understanding of the whole, or the main argument; and *third,* we shall single out a few special problems that emerge in the exegesis of the text and which have special bearing upon our thinking about Israel today as well as upon our understanding of the gospel of God's righteousness. Thus we are not only talking about the future of Israel, but also about Paul's basic understanding of God's grace.

The Development of Thought in Romans 9-11

First, we need to pay attention to *the change of mood* between chs 8 and 9. It could not be more dramatic. At the end of ch 8 Paul is walking on heavenly heights, but at the beginning of ch 9 he is "sorrowful unto death." In ch 8, vv 31ff., he bursts with joy as he contemplates God's gift in Jesus Christ: if God did not spare his own son, he will also give us all things with him. If God is on our side, nobody shall prevail against us. "I am sure," Paul says, that neither death, nor life, nor angels, nor principalities, nor things present, nor things to come, nor powers, nor height, nor depth, nor anything else in all creation, will be able to separate us from the love of God in Christ Jesus our Lord (8:38–39).

In the immediately following sentences, i.e., in 9:1ff., Paul confesses that he has "great sorrow and unceasing anguish in his heart" and that he could wish to be accursed and cut off from Christ, the very same Christ who is the gift of God's love from whom nothing can cut us off. The exegete cannot overlook the fact that this text is loaded with intense feelings and overpowering emotions, so much so that the weight of the mystery of Israel can pull the apostle down from the heavenly heights of union with God and his love, down into hellish condemnation and separation from God in Christ, to be propelled upwards again to the heights of the knowledge of God, which were awesome mountaintops even for Paul:

> O the depth of the riches and wisdom and knowledge of God! How unsearchable are his judgments and how inscrutable his ways! (11:33)

If one is unwilling to take Paul's talk of a "mystery" (11:25) and of the "unsearchable judgments" and "inscrutable ways" (11:33) as clumsy, evasive, illusory, or even artificial answers to the problem, then one is forced to grant that in the face of God's mystery Paul must inevitably come to the limits of his ability to explain God's ways, despite the vigor of his thinking and argumentation. When he tries to explain what defies rational analysis, his examples and illustrations, even when drawn from Old Testament scriptures, illuminate but also obscure, clarify but also lead the reader astray on detours, provide partial answers to known problems and at the same time raise unforeseen new problems.

The drastic change of mood between (a) the end of ch 8 and the beginning of ch 9, and (b) between the beginning of ch 9 and the end of ch 11, should not keep us from trying to follow the thoughts of Paul. Quite the contrary, it gives us reason to follow Paul's reflections very closely, because only if we do that shall we be able to see the contours of the mystery Paul is talking about. The change of mood makes us wonder whether what is involved here is not a "gut feeling" on the part of Paul which he seeks to express when faced with a baffling problem; or perhaps it is a profound, very deeply rooted conviction of Paul that has been challenged by the facts of history and which Paul now seeks to justify and to maintain in spite of some evidence to the contrary.

The issue Paul is struggling with is not immediately and clearly identified. Already at the beginning of ch 9 we need to read between the lines: Paul has great sorrow and unceasing anguish in his heart because Israel does not accept the gospel of Jesus Christ by faith. That this is the issue becomes clear from 9:31 onward. The rejection of the gospel by Israel is especially painful to Paul because it is the future of his own people which is at stake. Though Paul identifies them as his "kinsmen by race" (9:3), he applies to them the same word with which he addresses his fellow-Christians, namely, "brothers." These "brothers" of Paul had been specially prepared for the reception of the gospel (9:4–5):

—they bear the particular name which God gave to Jacob (Gen 32:28f.);

—they have been given the status of sons (υἱοθεσία);

—to them belongs the glory (δόξα probably means the manifestation of God's presence);

—the covenants (διαθῆκαι in the plural points to the acts of renewal and the covenant faithfulness of God);

—the giving of the law (νομοθεσία can stand for the "Torah" itself,[1] but more precisely it means the acts of lawgiving);[2]

—the cult (λατρεία = cultic service);

—the promises (cf. Rom 15:8: "For I tell you that Christ became a servant to the circumcised to show God's truthfulness, in or-

1. C. E. B. Cranfield, *A Critical and Exegetical Commentary on the Epistle to the Romans,* ICC (Edinburgh: T. & T. Clark, 1979) 2:463, and U. Wilckens, *Der Brief an die Römer* (Röm. 6–11), EKKNT 6 (Einsiedeln/Koln: Benziger Verlag; Neukirchen-Vluyn: Neukirchener Verlag, 1980) 2:188 A 828.

2. E. Käsemann, *Commentary on Romans,* G. Bromiley, trans. and ed. (Grand Rapids: Eerdmans, 1980) 247; O. Kuss, *Der Römerbrief. Dritte Lieferung Röm. 8:19–11:36* (Regensburg: Verlag Friedrich Pustet, 1978) 677; U. Luz, *Das Geschichtsverständnis des Paulus,* Beiträge zur evangelischen Theologie 49 (Munich: Chr. Kaiser Verlag, 1968) 272; O. Michel, *Der Brief an die Römer* KEK (Göttingen: Vandenhoeck & Ruprecht, 1966) 295.

der to confirm *the promises* given to the patriarchs" and
Rom 3:2: the Jews are entrusted with "the oracles of God");

—the patriarchs;

—the Messiah comes from the Jewish race as regards his human
descent (cf. Rom 1:3).

Israel thus characterized is distinguished by the kinship, the
blood relationship, which exists among the Jews; they are kinsmen by race (9:3). They are seen here as an ethnic entity. On
the other hand, the characteristics Paul enumerates do not have
their basis in the Jewish σάρξ; they are not inherent in the race,
rather they are the "notae" of God's election.[3] All these
"marks" are what they are through *God's* action, *his* initiative,
and *his* free choosing. And it is through this choice of God,
who is one, that Paul is related with Gentile Christians and *also*
with Jews as his "brothers."

The point of departure for Paul's reflections in Romans 9–11,
the life-setting in which the problem causing Paul so much sorrow and anguish arises, is the past history of his own people, a
past characterized by God's gracious turning to Israel. And because it was *God's* gracious initiative, this past has potential for
the future: Israel has been prepared for a future with God. This
is the thrust of the opening verses in ch 9, a theme that Paul has
hinted at already at the very beginning of the whole epistle:
"The gospel of God was promised beforehand through God's
prophets in the Holy Scriptures, the gospel concerning his son,
who was descended from David according to the flesh" (1:1–4).

Would it now be possible to argue: Because Israel did not permit itself to be led into God's future, its past has really become
a matter of the past without potential for the future? This thought
is not unthinkable: Israel is capable of denying itself as *God's
people*. It is indeed conceivable that Israel refuses to fulfill the
role that God has given it. Israel might run away from God. The
question, though, remains whether God lets it go! *It is not just
a question about Israel, it is also a question about God.* The
question of the integrity of Israel as God's people is simultaneously the question of the integrity of the electing God. If Israel
really allows its past, full of potential for the future, to degen-
erate into mere chronicles, should one then draw the conclu-

3. Wilckens, *Der Brief,* 2:187.

sion that God has come to his wit's end, that he has started something that he cannot finish? If Israel should disappear from the stage of history, would this also mean that God has abdicated as the Lord of history, at least as far as his plan is concerned? The question of Israel becomes the question of "theodicy." And because God is dealing with believing and unbelieving people, and not with puppets, it becomes also a question concerning "the paradox reality of election."[4] The question is simply this: How will God come to terms with his stiffnecked people who so skillfully run past their own salvation? In the history of theology the question is known to us as the problem of the relationship between the will of God and the freedom of humanity. Paul's reflection on the future of Israel is a case study of this perennial problem which runs through both Testaments and through almost two millennia of Christian thinking without ever having received a satisfactory answer on the rational level. It is fascinating to watch Paul as he tries to give his answer, an answer, however, which rests ultimately on his *faith and hope* and not on a rational, conceptual solution of the "paradox reality of Israel's election."

Commentators are agreed, by and large, that Romans 9–11 is best divided into three main sections, while the grouping of smaller text units can vary:

(1) 9:6–29 deal with God, the freedom of his election;

(2) 9:30–10:21 deal with Israel, the obstinacy of its rebellion against God;

(3) 11:1–32(36) present a solution to the problem of Israel's relationship to its God, the miracle of Israel's eschatological salvation.

Romans 9:6–29: The Freedom of God's Election

Paul's basic thesis concerning the question of Israel, as the apostle treats that question in Romans 9–11, is stated in 9:6a: "it is not as though the word of God had failed." The expression used here, namely, ὁ λόγος τοῦ θεοῦ ("the word of God"), reminds us of 3:2: Israel has been privileged to hear the word of

---

4. This is the heading which Wilckens, ibid., 2:181 has given to these three chapters.

God; it was entrusted with τὰ λόγια τοῦ θεοῦ. Since Paul uses λόγος (τοῦ θεοῦ), ἐπαγγελία ["promise"] (τοῦ θεοῦ) (9:6, 8, 9; 15:8), and πρόθεσις ["counsel"] (τοῦ θεοῦ) (8:28; 9:11) synonymously, one will be inclined to think of God's promise and counsel of salvation when one reads 9:6a; however, the use of (ὁ λόγος τοῦ θεοῦ in the singular is striking: obviously, Paul is not only concerned about the fulfillment of a very particular promise, but rather about the trustworthiness of *all* of God's pronouncements. May one trust God and his pronouncements? Or does he say *yes* today and *no* tomorrow? "For this reason three questions interact and overlap inseparably in what follows: the meaning of Israel's history, the validity of the promise, and the faithfulness and truth of God."[5] In the immediate context "it involves the specific promises to Israel, as in the λόγια τοῦ θεοῦ in 3:2,"[6] but behind that there lies the fundamental question of the reliability of the God of Israel as God, as the God also of the church of Jesus Christ and as the Creator and Redeemer of all.

The first sub-section (Rom 9:6b–13) offers two illustrations from the time of the patriarchs, to make the point that in God's action *election means also selection.*[7] The *election* of Isaac meant that one of the two sons of Abraham was *selected*; God elected Isaac and not Ishmael. The second illustration is even clearer: from the children of Isaac, God *elected* Jacob, and this meant that God *selected* one of the twin brothers. Nothing could illustrate better the *freedom* of God's choosing. This freedom existed already when Isaac was elected; the election of Jacob instead of Esau underlines again that God's πρόθεσις, his "counsel" or "purpose," emerges out of God's freedom. God's purpose lasts and continues according to God's own good pleasure (κατ' ἐκλογὴν; RSV "because of his call;" 9:11).

That Israel is Israel is due to nothing else than God's free grace. The consequence for our understanding of the phenomenon of Israel is that we must ask, Who is the true bearer of the promise? Not every descendant of Abraham is Abraham's true child; not every descendant of Abraham is God's child. Only the children of the promise are acknowledged as Abraham's

5. Käsemann, *Romans,* 261.
6. Ibid., 262.
7. Cf. Wilckens, *Der Brief,* 1:191.

"seed" (9:6b–8). It should be noted that in 9:8 ("the children of the promise are reckoned as descendants") Paul uses the verb that he consistently employs when he says that God "reckons" humankind's faith as "righteousness" (e.g., Rom 4:22–25). λο-γίζεται ("it is reckoned") points to a divine, juridical act: God declares humanity to be something it is not in itself.[8] "The apostle's concern is that the promise is not handed down immanently nor continued physically. It must be spoken and confirmed time and time again."[9]

If Paul's two illustrations in 9:6b–13 are meant to substantiate the main thesis, namely, that "it is not as though the word of God had failed" (9:6a), one might expect Paul now to continue with his argument by saying: though God's word to Israel has not become effective in the life of *all* Israelites, it has shown its effect among some of them, among the true Israelites, the true bearers of the promise. However, this line of thought is not drawn out until we get to ch 11, where in v 5 Paul makes this point: "So too at the present time there is a remnant κατ' ἐκ-λογὴν χάριτος = according to the choice of his grace." Between 9:13 and ch 11 Paul takes up other questions. But before we go on with these, it should be clearly recognized that in 9:6–13 Paul has taken issue with the thinking of his Jewish contemporaries. Because it was a fundamental creed in late Judaism that membership in Israel is gained by birth, Rom 9:6–13 must be understood as Paul's radical criticism of Israel's *claim* to divine election. Paul has made the point that there is nothing in the Jewish "flesh" that establishes a claim upon God's favor. On the contrary, Israel is God's chosen people *only* because of God's undeserved grace. And in this grace God is free. The corollary of this is that, according to Paul, one cannot deny the *possibility* of the rejection of a part of Israel. If God is free to choose the bearers of his promise, he is free to elect and to reject; he has the right to maintain the freedom of his election in the present and in the future as he did in the past. The problem of an emerging dichotomy between the people of Israel and the people of God comes into focus (9:6b). But Paul does not draw the conclusion that in the case of Israel physical descent does not matter at all. This would contradict 9:4–5, the enumeration

8. Cf. Wilckens, ibid., 2:192.
9. Käsemann, *Romans,* 262; also cited by Wilckens, ibid., 2:191.

of the "marks of Israel." In 9:6b–7 Paul maintains the continuity between the historical and the true Israel for part of the
people. "The context forces us to attribute the presence of a
true Israel within Judaism (cf. 4:11ff.; Gal 4:21ff.) purely to
God's electing."[10]

> If the people as the bearer of the promise is differentiated from the
> totality of its members . . . , one has to ask where and how this
> people appears. Is there in fact a continuity of the promise in
> earthly Israel which, however, is not sustained or guaranteed by the
> people as such but solely by the acting God? If so, then God is in
> truth this continuity and Israel is simply the earthly sphere chosen
> by him.[11]

The second sub-section (Rom 9:14–29) continues with the
theme of God's freedom in his selecting election in a dialogical
confrontation with contradicting objections. Verse 14 takes up
an objection that in the emphasis on divine freedom there lies
a threat to justice. And in v 29 the apostle responds to the res-
ervation that his interpretation of divine election destroys human responsibility.[12] From v 22 on Paul adds another thought:
when God calls the Gentiles to salvation, he does it out of the
same electing freedom that he has manifested in Israel. Let us
briefly deal with these three ideas.

Romans 9:14–18. Is there injustice on God's part? What sort
of "injustice" is meant? Cranfield holds that in trying to think
things through Paul poses a rhetorical question occasioned by
9:11, i.e., by the assertion that God's free electing is not dependent on human works and humanity's inherent qualifications,
but rather originates in God's own grace.[13] On the other hand,
Wilckens is of the opinion that Paul is involved in a very real discussion of a highly explosive matter.[14] The issue was broached
already in 3:5: Paul's Jewish dialogue partner raises the question: "If our wickedness serves to show the justice of God,
what shall we say? That God is unjust to inflict wrath on us?"
That's the way Paul formulates the question, and the assumption is that the opposing Jew makes the point: If Paul's interpre-

---

10. Käsemann, *Romans,* 263.
11. Ibid.
12. Cf. Michel, *Der Brief,* 305.
13. Cranfield, *Romans,* 2:482.
14. Wilckens, *Der Brief,* 2:199.

tation of God's election should be correct, especially the view that God, seemingly arbitrarily and without respect to birth and merit, elects some and rejects others, instead of bringing salvation to *all* Israelites, then God's covenant righteousness is radically put in question in its character as saving righteousness.

I am inclined to agree with Wilckens. Paul's interpretation of Israel's election as being totally based on God's inexplicable freedom divests Israel of all security based on race. For the Jewish opponent, Paul's argument is tantamount to a denial of the reality of God's covenant with Israel. Paul considers this a wrong inference from his understanding of election. He argues that the God of Israel, the Lord of the covenant, the electing God is no other than the Creator God. God's justice must be seen in conjunction with the rights of the Creator. To put it plainly: according to Paul, God can act as he chooses, and his acting cannot be measured or judged by any *human* standard of justice; rather it is just and always establishes justice. To get this point across is the purpose of the quotation in 9:15. This is the vantage point from which we must look at Paul's argument and not from any doctrine of predestination.[15] What justice is, is not measured by man's striving toward *his* ideal of justice; rather, it is determined by God's will and action, and—as 9:16 repeats—by God's *mercy.* When God acts in this way or in that way, there is no injustice in him. Justice is to be seen in whichever way God manifests his godhead, be it in mercy or in the hardening of human hearts. "He has mercy upon whomever he wills, and he hardens the heart of whomever he wills" (9:18). This is a "hard saying."[16]

Romans 9:19–21. If God has mercy upon whomever he wills, and if he hardens the heart of whomever he wills (9:18), why does he still accuse us? Isn't *he* responsible for the hardening of our hearts? Isn't his will irresistible? (9:18–19). Paul counters this objection not by trying to relate the freedom of God and human responsibility but by simply quashing the criticism.

15. Cf. H. Schlier, *Der Römerbrief,* HTKNT 6 (Freiburg/Basel/Wren: Herder, 1977) 295.

16. Cf. Hugo Grotius, 1583–1645, who argued that "natural law" is valid "etsi deus non daretur," even if God does not exist; however, Grotius did not see any contradiction between God's will and natural law, and his point of departure was that of Paul: what God wills is just, not vice-versa.

Paul strikes down the objection. A human being cannot become God's accuser, for right is not a neutral norm for the creature but is given only by the Creator, whose own right is coincident with his creative freedom.[17]

It is obvious that for Paul divine freedom and divine action do not do away with humankind's responsibility to God; but he does not help us here by providing us with a "thought model" that would enable us to relate the two in such a way that the integrity of both, the divine and the human action, can be maintained. He simply says that in this matter human beings and God cannot be considered equal partners.

Romans 9:22–29. Thus far Paul's reflections about God and the freedom of his election were related to Israel: the elected and believing Israelites and the hardened and disbelieving Jews; and the true Israel as the bearer of God's promise and the Jewish race. In 9:24 Paul widens the circle of the people of God so as to include the Gentiles. This widening of the perspective has a double effect. On the one hand, it heightens the paradox of divine election; on the other, it eases the problem of God's seemingly arbitrary electing and rejecting. It eases this problem at least from one perspective by suggesting that as regards humankind as a whole, there is a hidden blessing in the hardening of the majority of the Jews since because of their rejection of their messiah, the gospel of God has come to the Gentiles. Paul has more to say about this in 9:30ff. Let us stay with 9:22–29 for a moment.

In the history of exegesis and systematic theology, 9:22–29 has provided much of the basis for the development of a doctrine of "double predestination." However, I think it would be wrong to understand what Paul is saying here and in the immediately preceding verses as a defence for a despotic divinity whose arbitrariness is uncurbed. One cannot overlook the predestinarian language of Paul that may derive from the apocalyptic movement as represented in Qumran.[18] Yet in view of vv 22–24 one wishes to emphasize that Paul's interest does not focus on a "double predestination" but rather on God's saving

17. Käsemann, *Romans,* 269.

18. Cf. Luz, *Das Geschichtsverständnis,* 228ff. and C. Müller, *Gottes Gerechtigkeit und Gottes Volk. Eine Untersuchung zu Römer 9–11,* FRLANT 86 (Göttingen: Vandenhoeck & Ruprecht, 1964): 77ff.

history grounded in God's promise.[19] Schlier says quite correctly that Paul's

> main concern is to impress upon the reader the superior and incomprehensible reality of God and the reality of the incomprehensible in God the Creator and Almighty Lord, and at the same time the unquestionable dependence of man and his history upon this incomprehensible, not disposable, not accusable, free and self-glorious God. And all of this is always controlled by the thought of the great mystery of Israel which has not been forgotten.[20]

One might add that already here the reader senses something of the "inscrutable ways" of God (11:33) when the Creator God forms vessels of wrath, but then bears them up with much patience, and when, above all, the winding ways of the caring and providing Lord of history bring to light the riches of God's glory. Käsemann suggests that "predestination is not despotic caprice when it establishes salvation history. Its soteriological function is just as constitutive as its connection with the word of God which works creatively and directs it."[21]

Romans 9:22-29 helps us to understand that Paul appeals to God's sovereignty, the freedom of his election, for two reasons: first, it is the basis that makes possible the calling of the Gentiles along with the believers from among the Israelites (9:23f), and second, it is the basis from which Paul can speak of the reality of the wrath of God upon his stiffnecked people and can reject the exclusive claim of Israel as the singular people of God. The Scripture quotations in 9:25-29 illustrate the paradox of the unexpected, miraculous calling of the Gentiles and the rejection of the majority of the ancient people of God.

Concerning the future of Israel, Romans 9 is first of all a confirmation of the validity of God's promise to his chosen people Israel, yet in a clearly qualified and limited sense in that Paul contests the *claim* of Israel to salvation based on its election. God's salvation always remains his *free* gift. Secondly, God grants his salvation in unexpected ways also to those who were not his people. As the God who "calls into existence the things that do not exist" (4:17), the Creator molds the community that shares in his salvation out of those who were *not* his children

---

19. Cf. Michel, *Der Brief,* 306, 311.
20. Schlier, *Der Römerbrief,* 300.
21. Käsemann, *Romans,* 273.

(9:26). With these insights, however, the mystery of the paradox reality of salvation has not yet been uncovered.

Romans 9:30–10:21: Israel—the
Obstinacy of Its Rebellion against God

Romans 9:30–33 appears to be the conclusion to ch 9. On
the other hand, it reads like an introduction to ch 10.[22] The
connection with the former is given by the reflection on the addition of the Gentiles; the connection with the latter is provided by the resumption of *the theme of God's righteousness,*
which is now added to the subject of the freedom of God in his
actions, the sovereignty of God, of which Paul has spoken thus
far. The decisive thought here is that *God's people have an
open future before them only when they find their way to the
righteousness that is obtained through faith alone.* Israel is
striving for God's righteousness on the basis of works; the Gentiles, however, have attained it—the true (!) righteousness—on
the basis of faith. One needs to define this contrast between
faith and works still more precisely because another paradox
comes to the fore here: The Gentiles did not pursue righteousness
(ἔθνη τὰ μὴ διώκοντα δικαιοσύνην) and yet they received it
(κατέλαβεν); the Israelites, on the other hand, did pursue a
"law of righteousness" but never attained to it (νόμον οὐκ ἔφθασεν). The Gentiles received salvation without the gift of the
law Paul mentioned in 9:4; the Jews who lived possessing the
law missed its true intention when they thought that a sinner
could become righteous by doing the works of the law. As long
as Israel remains in this state of rebellion, the Torah does not remain that saving gift that the Jews believe they possess in it.

The quotation in v 33 shows that Paul draws such conclusions from the vantage point of the Christ event. Christ himself
is the stone that makes men and women stumble. In the encounter with him it becomes clear what "God's righteousness"
really is all about and why Israel, when it rejects its Messiah, a
man of its race (9:5), does not know what to do with the gift
of the law (9:4). Resistance to Christ is, simultaneously, resistance to the Torah.[23] The refusal of faith in Christ, the stone

22. Michel, *Der Brief,* 319.
23. Wilckens, *Der Brief,* 2:216.

which God has laid in Zion, constitutes Israel's guilt and causes it to stumble.

Romans 10:1–21 corroborate Israel's guilt: God did not fail to extend his calling invitation, and therefore Israel must be held responsible for refusing to heed this call. At the end of this passage we might expect to find the verdict: Israel is finished. God has rejected it. The rebellious resistance of Israel against God must be understood precisely as resistance to God's righteousness, a righteousness that is received by faith and not by works. This theme was posed already with vv 30–33 in ch 9. In 10:1–13 another attempt is made to expound the δικαιοσύνη τοῦ θεοῦ. In fact, 10:1–13 summarizes in succinct formulations what Paul had explicated at some length in 3:21 to 4:25:

—The righteousness Paul is talking about is not self-righteousness, rather it is the righteousness "that comes from God" (RSV), it is "God's way of righteousness" (NEB), "God's way of putting people right" (GNB) (10:3).

—It does not come from the law (as the fulfillment of its commands; 10:5), but it comes from Jesus Christ in whom we believe (10:4).

The sentence τέλος γὰρ νόμου Χριστὸς is usually—and correctly, I think—translated as "Christ is the end of the law" (RSV) or it is rendered, with the same meaning, by the verbal formulation

"Christ ends the law" (NEB)

"Christ has brought the law to an end" (GNB)

or, with a change of subject,

"the law has come to an end with Christ" (JB).

Most commentators advocate this rendering.[24] The suggestions of Cranfield and Wilckens to translate τέλος by "the goal, the intention, the real meaning and substance" and "the final goal" are linguistically defensible but exegetically untenable.[25]

24. Cf. Michel, *Der Brief,* 326; Schlier, *Der Römerbrief,* 311; Käsemann, *Romans,* 282–85.

25. Cranfield, *Romans,* 2:519; Wilckens, *Der Brief,* 2:222f; see the immediate context of 9:31ff. and 10:4ff.; the epistle as a whole: 3:21; 5:20; 7:1ff.; 8:2f; the theology of the apostle in Gal, 2 Cor 3, and Phil 3; Käsemann, *Romans,* 282–83.

—The true righteousness is revealed in the Gospel in whose proclamation the exalted Christ makes himself known on earth.
Faith "does not . . . have to discover Christ because he is always
on the scene before us already in the word of preaching."[26]

—The righteousness of God is in reality wherever Jesus the Risen
Lord is believed and confessed (10:9–10).

—"God's way of putting people right" is born witness to in the
Scriptures but it is not bound to Israel; also the Greeks who confess the one Lord are put right by God through faith (10:11–13).

The second part of ch 10 (10:14–21) is meant to prove that the
rejection of God's righteousness, which is revealed in the gospel,
is inexcusable. The questions in vv 14–15a replace apodictic
statements. Israel could not "call upon God," "believe," "hear,"
and "preach" as long as there was no mission. But now messengers have been sent out. A justifying faith is possible because
the kerygma has been declared, has been made audible through
the messengers whom God has sent: "How beautiful are the
feet of those who preach good news!" (10:15). The author has
in mind the moment of the eschatological realization of God's
promise. The message can be heard; it is ultimately the word of
the exalted Lord himself (10:17) who makes the hearing of his
word possible through the preaching of his messengers, and it
is from such hearing that "faith comes" (10:17).

For the Israelites, too, hearing has become a concrete possibility because the voice of proclamation has gone out to all the
earth (10:18). The question, Is it not possible that they don't believe because they haven't heard anything? must be answered:
No, this cannot be the explanation for their lack of faith. Indeed, it is not a "lack" of faith; it is a refusal to believe, for they
did have opportunity to hear. But one can go on and ask: Perhaps, they did hear, but then did not comprehend what they
heard? (10:19). This excuse is also of no help in avoiding the verdict, "Israel is guilty." Israel understood very well. It knows
what it is rejecting. The quotations in vv 19 and 21, taken from
Dt 32:21 and Isa 52:2, complain about the unfaithfulness of
God's people; Paul addresses them directly to his Jewish contemporaries. The citation in the middle, in v 20, taken from Isa
65:1, is applied to the Gentile Christians: God let himself be

26. Käsemann, *Romans,* 290.

found by those who did not seek him; and he wants to make the Israelites jealous of believing non-Jews (10:19). However, God is holding out his hands for Israel without success. Israel doesn't listen, or rather, it contradicts what it hears (10:21). Israel is λαὸς ἀπειθοῦντος καὶ αντιλέγοντος. The contradiction shows itself in "disobedience," the fundamental human sin. The consequence is that Israel forfeits God's righteousness and thus its own salvation.

Romans 11:1–36: The Miracle of Israel's Eschatological Salvation—A Solution to the Problem of Israel's Rebellion Against God

In Romans 10 unbelieving Israel has been pinned down. There is no way to escape the verdict "Guilty!" Should we now draw the conclusion that God has rejected his people? The question has been with us from the beginning of ch 9. The apostle replies with an emphatic "*no!* Even the unbelieving Israel continues to bear the marks of her divine election." Paul states the reasons for his rebuttal of the notion that God is through with Israel in 11:1–4:

—First of all, and quite simply, Paul himself is a genuine Israelite. In his own person Paul furnishes a proof that God has not rejected his people (11:1).

—Second, Paul draws a conclusion from his own person to the fate of Israel as a whole, and he justifies this conclusion with a Scripture quotation. From the story of Elijah, the apostle concludes for his own time that a "remnant" has been left over, not because of their own merits but by the choice of God's grace (κατ' ἐκλογὴν χάριτος, 11:5).

However, we cannot overlook the fact that (1) a "remnant" is a part and not the whole; and (2) the "remnant" is identical with the Jewish-Christian church. Thus far Paul has provided evidence only for the assertion that God has not rejected *all* of Israel.

After Paul has repeated that even the salvation of that "remnant" is nothing but divine grace (11:6), he renews his question: What then? Where do we stand now? Since God's all sufficient grace has created only the eschatological remnant, Israel has attained the goal only *in this remnant*. Thus the reader needs to distinguish between the "remnant," the "elect" (λεῖμμα =

ἐκλογή), on the one hand, and the "rest" (λοιποί) on the other hand. The "remnant" signifies God's faithfulness to Israel. It does not rest upon the virtues or accomplishments of the symbolic "seven thousand men" (11:4), but rather on God's unfathomable grace. The "rest," however, the unbelieving Jews, still adhere to the principle of the law and strive after righteousness by way of merits. This is their own guilt and a divine hardening of their hearts at the same time (οἱ δὲ λοιποὶ ἐπωρώθησαν, 11:7). Once again the question of God's freedom or caprice emerges. If the salvation of a "remnant" has become possible through an absolutely free act of God's grace, how then will God's sovereignty show itself in his dealings with the "rest" (λοιποί)? If the existence of the Jewish-Christian church demonstrates that God did not reject Israel *in toto,* and if the Jewish-Christian community owes its existence solely to God's grace, may one then not also hope and look forward to an act of free divine grace in God's relationship to the (λοιποί)?

The choice of the word "hardening" in 11:7 has left room for this sort of question, and in 11:11 Paul poses it directly: "Did the rest stumble *so as to fall?*" After all, one may stumble and regain one's balance, or stumble and stand up again. Paul resists the thought of Israel's stumbling with the result of a final fall, a fall without rising. And he does it with an argument from salvation history: through the hardening of Israel salvation has come to the Gentiles. In this manner the "rest" play an eschatological role even in their hardening before Christ and his gospel, and from this Paul draws the conclusion that "the instrument of God's grace against its own will continues to be the object of this grace."[27]

But Paul does not stop here. Using a rabbinic exegetical method, the *qal-waḥomer* conclusion (πόσῳ μᾶλλον = "how much more" 11:12), Paul contemplates even greater blessings: "If their trespass means riches for the world, and if their failure means riches for the Gentiles, how much more will their full inclusion mean!" (11:12). The words "full inclusion" render the Greek πλήρωμα. πλήρωμα is to be understood as the sum, the full number, constituted by the λεῖμμα and the λοιποί, the remnant and the "rest." Paul is thinking of the time when the hitherto unbelieving and rebelling Jews will join their believing brothers

27. Ibid., 304.

and, thus, the number of the Israelites will be "full."[28]

One wonders where Paul finds the presupposition of this idea! The *qal-waḥomer* conclusion only makes the inference that *if* the failure of Israel, its falling short (τὸ ἥττημα = the deficit), brought with it such riches for the Gentiles, the full restoration of Israel as God's believing people will result in still greater blessings. But how does Paul know that there will be a restoration of Israel as a whole? Obviously, Paul already presupposes here the mystery of which he will speak in 11:25f.: "all Israel will be saved." That there will be a πλήρωμα of Israel seems to be an axiom in Paul's thinking. In any case, the point in v 12 is that "there will no longer be a distinction between the true and the false seed, the remnant and the people. In virtue of the promise given to it Judaism is an eschatological entity as πᾶς 'Ισραήλ, and it remains so even in judgment and against its own will."[29]

Before the time of the salvation of all Israel has arrived, the Gentile mission needs to be fulfilled. This is not as clear here as in Mk 13:10, but it is implied in the idea that the acceptance of the gospel by the Gentiles is meant to make Israel jealous (11:11) and it is said more or less *expressis verbis* later on in 11:25: "a hardening has come upon part of Israel, *until the full number of the Gentiles comes in.*" It can also be concluded from Paul's dating of the salvation of all Israel. We shall deal with this point later in another context.

As regards Paul's reasoning in favor of the salvation of all Israel, we need to pay attention also to 11:16:

> If the dough offered as first fruits is holy, so is the whole lump; and if the root is holy, so are the branches.

This verse is undoubtedly meant to illustrate the expectation of salvation for *all* Israel. Through the election of the patriarchs, Israel as a whole has been sanctified; and as the patriarchs represent the roots of the tree Israel, so all Israelites, representing branches of this tree, are sanctified and have a share in the election of the Fathers (note the references to the patriarchs in 9:5

---

28. Cf. on this Wilckens, *Der Brief,* 2:243; Schlier, *Der Römerbrief,* 329ff.; Käsemann, *Romans,* 304 with G. Delling, *TDNT,* 6:298–305, s.v. πλήρωμα; Cranfield, *Romans,* 2:558; Michel, *Der Brief,* 345 (*apokalyptische Vollzahl*).

29. Käsemann, *Romans,* 305.

and 11:28).[30] How much weight these two illustrations in 11:16 can carry and to which extent they furnish plausible *reasons* for a hope in the salvation of all Israel, is another matter. Paul is surely not arguing on the assumption that there is an immanent process of development in Israel and that Israel has a "natural" claim upon salvation; rather, Paul affirms the continuity of the sometimes hidden faithfulness of God in Israel's history, and the conversion of Israel stands beyond any doubt. Thus the exegete will be reluctant to press the illustrations as proofs; they furnish analogies for a reality which, for Paul, is grounded in God himself.[31]

Verses 17–24 form a coherent warning addressed to Gentile Christians. Paul uses the parable of the olive tree to call to humility those who were grafted into this tree as wild branches. They have no reason to exalt themselves above the original, natural branches which God has broken off. If God has accomplished the feat of engrafting wild branches, how much more (a *qal-waḥomer* conclusion, 11:24) easily will God graft the natural branches back into their own olive tree (11:25). In the overall context, the parable means nothing else than that the salvation of all Israel should not be considered more astonishing and surprising than the salvation of the Gentiles! And the lesson which the Gentile Christians need to draw from the parable is that if God dealt so severely with his own chosen people, then the former heathen have even greater reason to watch out: they too could be cut off if they do not continue in God's kindness (11:22).

In 11:25–32 Paul's reflections reach their climax. He reveals the mystery that determined his thinking from the beginning and that, in the narrower context in which it is explicitly stated, provides the reason for Paul's own expectation that the original branches will be grafted back into their own natural olive tree. The uncovering of the "mystery" (11:25) has its own paraenetic nuance that one should not overlook. Paul introduces the mystery with the words: "Lest you be wise in your own conceits" (11:25). He addresses himself to Gentiles (11:13), telling them that as Gentile Christians there is no reason for them to develop a spirit of elitism based on the consciousness of an exclusive

30. Cf. Schlier, *Der Römerbrief,* 332; Cranfield, *Romans,* 2:565; Wilckens, *Der Brief,* 2:246.

31. Cf. Cranfield, *Romans,* 2:565; Michel, *Der Brief,* 348.

status in redemptive history, and thus to look down upon the unbelieving Jews.[32] In his own wisdom and in his ways of free grace God has bound Israel and the church together in a remarkable manner. Israel was elected first. When the majority of the Jews failed to accept their Messiah, the gospel began to run its course among the Gentiles. When the full number of Gentiles have come in, all Israel will be saved (11:25–26). This interaction between Israel and the church is the theme of this passage. One may even ask whether this is not the very content of the "mystery." The "mystery" is not so much that "all Israel will be saved" (as we have noted earlier, the final conversion of all Israel seems to be presupposed by Paul throughout). Rather, the "mystery" has to do with the *manner* of Israel's salvation, the ways in which it will come about (11:26).

Paul has led up to the announcement of the "mystery" in a rather dramatic way. After having dealt with God's freedom in the election and selection of his people (9:6–29) and then with the obstinacy of Israel's rebellion against God (9:30–10:21), at the beginning of ch 11 the apostle finally poses the question that has forced itself upon the reader from the very beginning: "Has God rejected his people?" (11:1). Is God through with Israel? Is there no future for it? Paul's immediate reply is: "By no means! God has not rejected Israel. Look at me! God has chosen me, and I am an Israelite" (11:1). And then Paul continues: "I am not alone. As it was in the days of Elijah, so it is now: God, in his sheer grace, has preserved a remnant as you can see in the existence of the *Jewish*-Christian community" (11:2–6). However, this answer does not yet meet the question: But what about Israel *as a whole*? What is going to happen to all those Jews who have rejected their messiah and have not come to faith in Jesus Christ? Paul begins to deal with this issue concretely at 11:7. He says: "Those and others who have not come to faith are hardened" (11:7), and the meaning is: "They are *only* hardened." Paul does not use the word "only," but that this is the sense of 11:7 becomes clear in vv 11ff. The Jews have stumbled but this does not mean that they have fallen flat on their faces and can never rise again. The truth is that God continues to use Israel, and it is the God *of grace* who uses Israel. However stubborn Israel's rebellion may be, God has not come to the end of

---

32. Cf. Wilckens, *Der Brief,* 2:252, n. 1125.

his wits; the resources of his wisdom have not been depleted. The fact is that the hardening of Israel has had a surprisingly beneficial side-effect, and this is God's doing: through the rebellion of Israel salvation is coming to the Gentiles (which was the purpose of Israel's election in the first place, Gen 12:3; 17:4, etc.). And God is capable of doing still greater things with Israel and with all the nations. Romans 11:12 spells this out: "If the failure of Israel proved to be so beneficial for the rest of humankind, how much greater things will accompany the final salvation of all Israel!" Since this sounds a bit mysterious, we shall return to the question concerning what these greater things are concretely. We note, though, that here in 11:12 as well as in 11:15, 16, 23, 24 the salvation of all Israel is *presupposed*. This speaks in favor of the thesis that the "mystery" has to do not with the salvation of Israel as such, but specifically with its manner. The announcement of the "mystery" in 11:25 adds to what has already been said, only the insight that the date of the salvation of all Israel will coincide with the completion of the Gentile mission, the "coming in" of their "full number." Israel's salvation will not happen earlier. But then it will happen. The time of the hardening of their hearts is limited by that eschatological hour.

In the light of this coordination of Gentile mission and salvation of all Israel we can understand the interaction between the two as pictured in vv 28–32. Israel's enmity against God proved to be—humanly speaking—an unforeseen blessing for the Gentiles (11:28, 30–31). On the other hand, God's love for Israel has not ceased because of their forefathers, more precisely because of God's promises to the patriarchs (11:28–29). If God has led the Gentiles from their disobedience to a life lived out of God's mercy, and if God has done that in his astounding wisdom through the disobedience of the Israelites, then the Jews will also be recipients of the same divine mercy that has been shown to the Gentiles (11:30–31). The sovereignty of the Creator and Redeemer, who is at work in and above human disobedience, is at work even in his hardening of human hearts for the final triumph of his mercy in the eschatological hour. "For God has consigned all men to disobedience, that he may have mercy upon all" (11:32).

The whole section of this epistle, chs 9–11, comes to its conclusion not with additional arguments in the defence of God's actions, but rather with a moving doxology, the praise of the God from whom and through whom and to whom are all things (11:33–38). "In the end God . . ." The last word in Paul's reflections on the future of Israel is not "great sorrow and unceasing anguish of heart" (9:2) but the ultimate triumph of a loving, merciful and incredibly wise God.

Understanding the Whole: The Main Problem and the Main Solution

The Main Problem

The overwhelming majority of the Jews do not respond positively to what the adherents of Jesus consider to be the decisive, completely unprecedented saving work of God through Jesus Christ. Does this rejection by Israel amount to the bankruptcy of Israel's God Yahweh?[33] In the language of Rom 9:6 the fundamental question is: "Has the word of God failed?" If this should be the case, God has abdicated; he is dead. However, not only would this be the end of Israel. It would also mean that there is no certainty about the salvation that is proclaimed in the gospel of God's Christ (Rom 1:1–4, 16–17; 8:31–39). If there is no reality to God's speaking, then the gospel of God (1:1) for which Paul has been set apart is also a λόγος τοῦ θεοῦ that has no substance to it.

> If the truth is that God's purpose with Israel has been frustrated, then what sort of a basis for Christian hope is God's purpose? And, if God's love for Israel (cf., e.g., Deut. 7:7f.; Jer. 31:3) has ceased, what reliance can be placed on Paul's conviction that nothing can separate us from God's love in Christ (v 38f)?[34]

The problem of Israel leads to a crisis in the image of God for both Jews and Christians. Both affirm to be the ἀγαπητοί of God (cf. Rom 8:38f.; 11:28), and both believe that God's love for them will never fail. From the viewpoint of the unconverted Jewish opponent of Paul the central issue could be seen as follows:

> Paul wants to, and needs to, give an answer to the fundamental objection of the Jewish partner who argues that the universal proclamation of salvation through the gospel for Jews and Gentiles has been bought at the price of the breaking of God's promise of election made to Israel; the thesis of the justification of all men as sin-

33. Kuss, *Der Römerbrief*, 3:928.
34. Cranfield, *Romans*, 2:447.

ners would be established on the broken foundation of redemptive history; therefore the Gospel could not possibly be anything but an empty word, the salvation proclaimed in it could not have any reality to it; the church gathered from the Jews and the Gentiles could only be a community of salvation without any ground of salvation; for the justice of God, which is being proclaimed in the Gospel, couldn't be anything but injustice, because it would no longer have anything to do with God's covenant righteousness for Israel. It is this complaint about the lack of reality in the Christians' talking about God and God's salvation as one great preposterous blasphemy that Paul has to counter, after in Romans 6–8 he has rejected the accusation that the Christians' righteousness is unreal. But since the latter accusation (dealt with in Rom. 6–8) is grounded in the former (dealt with in Rom. 9–11), the answer given by Paul in chs. 6–8 has strength only if Paul now succeeds in refuting the fundamental Jewish objection that if the Gospel were true it would mean the end of God's covenant faithfulness.[35]

Whether Rom 9:6 is meant to counter a Jewish objection to the gospel or whether it has in view those Gentile Christians who exalt themselves above the hardened Israelites (as is surely the case in 11:17–24), 9:6 and 11:29 and 32 show in any case that the whole section, Romans 9–11, is bracketed by the disturbing question whether the wholesome λόγος τοῦ θεοῦ is still valid. In 9:6 Paul asserts that the "word of God" has not failed; in 11:29 he makes the point that "the gifts and the call of God are irrevocable," and in 11:32 he goes even further by saying that "God has consigned all men to disobedience, that he may have mercy upon all." This last sentence hints at the solution Paul has to offer to the problem of Israel's future.

The Main Solution

The basic answer that Paul gives to the main question we have just sketched is simply this: in his own intricate ways God's salvation comes to both Jews and Gentiles. The failure of the Jews is a very serious matter, but—by God's totally undeserved mercy and completely unfathomable wisdom—Israel's failure does not result in complete disaster; not the rebellious Jew but the gracious God has the last word. Through Israel's rebellion the door to the Gentiles has been opened and the gospel takes its course among the nations. Their conversion will, in turn, awaken the jealousy of the unconverted Jews, and thus, in

35. Wilckens, *Der Brief,* 2:181ff.

God's eternal wisdom, "all" people, all Gentiles and Jews, will be brought into the realm of salvation in the manner in which Paul now reveals it to the readers of his epistle in Rome.[36]

This is the answer of Paul in broad outline. Thinking it through and spelling it out in some detail, the apostle explicates the theme of the "righteousness of God." He does it in the middle section, in 9:30–10:13. Theologically speaking, Paul sees the key to the troublesome question of Israel's future in the doctrine of justification. It is obvious, though, that this doctrine of justification is related to both Christology and redemptive history. We recall that the whole epistle begins with a christological statement that relates the mission of Christ to God's chosen people Israel:

> Paul, a servant of Jesus Christ, called to be an apostle, set apart for the gospel of God which he promised beforehand through his prophets in the holy scriptures, the gospel concerning his Son, who was descended from David according to the flesh and designated Son of God in power according to the Spirit of holiness by his resurrection from the dead, Jesus Christ our Lord (Rom 1:1–4; cf. also 15:8–9).

The christological statement of 1:1–4 is interpreted soteriologically in 1:16–17. The gospel which Paul proclaims is

> the power of God for salvation to everyone who has faith, to the Jew first and also to the Greek. For in it the righteousness of God is revealed through faith for faith.

The soteriological statement that follows in 3:21–26 is, in turn, given a christological basis. In Romans 9–11, then, it becomes clear that justification, rooted in Christ, has a historical dimension: God's justification of the sinner, God's righteousness, is the center of redemptive history, and redemptive history is the worldwide dimension of God's righteousness.[37] To be sure, the Pauline message of God's righteousness becomes concrete in the justification of the individual believer, but it cannot and must not be reduced to a matter between God and the individual soul (cf. Rom 4); it is a matter between God and humankind ("for everyone who believes" whether Jew or non-Jew; 1:16). But to say that justification has its worldwide dimension in redemptive history does not mean that this salvation history is an immanent process of development into which, at a definite point

---

36. Cf. Kuss, *Der Römerbrief,* 3:928.
37. Cf. Käsemann, *Romans,* 95 and 256.

or moment, justification can be fitted. "Rather justification retains its dominance even in face of and within the scheme of salvation history."[38] Paul faces the fact that

> The promise which has been given to Israel and the goal of God's
> saving counsel which is perceptible at present diverge. Hence Paul
> has to show that the divine promise is neither calculable nor a human privilege. Salvation history is not a process of continuous development. It is the history of the word which constantly goes forth
> afresh and accomplishes election and rejection. In this way the Jewish belief in election is transcended.[39]

Consequently, Paul starts and finishes with his understanding of God's righteousness, the undeserved justification of sinners, when he interprets the beginnings of Israel's history in the person of Abraham (Rom 4); when he reflects upon the present state of Israel, her rebellion against the gospel (Rom 9:6ff.; 11:5–10); and when he tells his readers what he anticipates as Israel's future (Rom 11:11–32).

Comments on Selected Questions

Two points which we have touched upon all too briefly call for further clarification: first, the question of the *time* of Israel's salvation. When will all Israel be saved? Second, the question of the *manner* of Israel's salvation. How will Israel be saved? Two contemporary issues, the question of the significance of the present state of Israel and the question of the mission to the Jews in our times, deserve mention as well. And finally, I should like to highlight once more the contribution that Romans 9–11 make to the understanding of God's righteousness and thus to our understanding of the epistle to the Romans and of one of the most important pillars of Paul's theology. Our very first question, though, has to be a hermeneutical one.

Did Paul change his mind and would he change it again?

There cannot be any doubt that according to Romans 9–11 Israel as a people has a future, a future blessed by God with his gift of salvation. What Paul has said in 9:6 and 11:11–16, 23–24, 26, 31–32 does not leave any doubt about that. It is equally clear, however, that Paul did not always think like that. In 1 Thes-

---

38. Ibid., 264.
39. Ibid., 273.

salonians, probably the earliest letter of Paul, we hear a very different voice (1 Thes 2:14–16):

> For you, brethren, became imitators of the churches of God in Christ Jesus which are in Judea; for you suffered the same things from your own countrymen as they did from the Jews, who killed both the Lord Jesus and the prophets, and drove us out, and displease God and oppose all men by hindering us from speaking to the Gentiles that they may be saved—so as always to fill up the measure of their sins. But God's wrath has come upon them εἰς τέλος.

Many of our modern translations have a footnote at the end of v 16 with a comment upon the meaning of εἰς τέλος. The RSV translates: "God's wrath has come upon them *at last.*" And its footnote says: "Or *completely,* or *for ever.*" The NEB does it the other way around: "and now retribution has overtaken them *for good and all.*" The footnote reads: "Or *now at last* retribution has overtaken them." Linguistically both translations are possible. The tone of the whole passage and the absence of any qualification of this verdict makes many commentators inclined to translate εἰς τέλος. by "for good," "for ever." Furthermore, this reading of 1 Thes 2:16 is frequently supported by reference to Gal 4:21–31. As regards their time of writing, the letter to the Galatians stands between 1 Thessalonians and Romans. The statement in Galatians is clearer in its negative verdict on Israel. Hagar symbolizes Mount Sinai, the earthly Jerusalem, Judaism, and slavery (Gal 4:24–25). Sarah represents the Jerusalem above, the free, the Christians. The Jews are rejected by God, they are excommunicated as it were; they have lost their heritage. The church alone is the heir:

> as at that time he who was born according to the flesh persecuted him who was born according to the Spirit, so it is now. But what does the Scripture say? "Cast out the slave and her son; for the son of the slave shall not inherit with the son of the free woman" (4:29–30 with ref. to Gen 21:10; cf. Wilckens II. 184f.).

The reader of this text is reminded of an equally harsh judgment upon the Jews, namely Jn 8:31ff. Jesus contests the claim of the Jews who are talking with him and calls them not sons of Abraham but sons of the devil (Jn 8:39, 44). The Gospels of Matthew and of Luke do not use such drastic language, but for the first evangelist the church is surely the "true Israel," replacing the old covenant people, and for Luke there does not seem to exist any hope of a conversion of Israel (see Acts 28:25–29).

In Romans 9–11 Paul does not draw such conclusions. Here

he hangs on to the lasting validity of the divine promise to Israel (9:6; 11:29), and he expects that the natural branches, which have been cut off temporarily, will be grafted back into their own natural olive tree (11:24). Romans 9–11 know nothing of a replacement of Israel by the church. One could possibly say that for a limited time the people of God will be represented by a part of Israel *together with* the Gentile Christians, but it is not forgotten that at the end all of Israel will be "brought in" and will make the people of God complete. In his comments on Rom 9:1–4 Käsemann characterizes Israel, whose marks Paul enumerates, as the covenant people, whose life is grounded in God's election, who are historically determined by the promise and embraced by redemptive history; as such they are "virtually sacramentally stigmatized."[40]

> The theology and the historical situation of the apostle do not allow him to be satisfied with the solution of later Gentile Christianity that the promise is fulfilled spiritually, namely in the church. . . . This statement is not renounced. Yet it is not enough, because for Paul the church does not simply replace Israel. It is not a new thing with no dimension of depth historically, which then becomes merely a historic entity. The dialectical relation of promise and gospel would thereby lose its seriousness. . . . The problem of Israel after the flesh cannot be shoved aside if one is not to end up with Marcion.[41]

There is good reason, then, not to base one's appreciation of Paul's view of Israel's future on 1 Thes 2:14–16 and Gal 4:21–31 at the expense of Romans 9–11. The latter is Paul's later word on the subject. Is it conceivable that Paul would have changed his mind once more? There are several reasons for this question: (1) Romans was written around A.D. 55, and this means 15 years before the destruction of Jerusalem, the loss of the Jewish homeland and the dispersion of its population. Would this historical fact have an influence upon Paul's expectations for Israel? (2) The return of Christ did not take place in the immediate future as Paul expected it while writing the letter to the Romans. In 13:11f. Paul admonishes the Christians in Rome:

> Besides this you know what hour it is, how it is full time now for you to wake from sleep. For salvation is nearer to us now than when we first believed; the night is far gone, the day is at hand. Let us then cast off the works of darkness and put on the armor of light.

40. See original German editing: *An die Römer,* HNT 8a (Tübingen: J. C. B. Mohr, 1973) 247. The English translation, (259) reads "is marked sacramentally."
41. Ibid., 261.

The expectation of an imminent parousia is reflected also in the use of the word νῦν in 11:31: "they have now been disobedient in order that by the mercy shown to you they also may *now* receive mercy." For Paul the eschatological hour has come so close that soon the full number of the Gentiles will have been brought in and the parousia will take place.[42] (3) Since 1948 there exists a modern state of Israel. Would its establishment have any influence upon Paul's thinking if Paul were our contemporary?

These questions are legitimate and refer to historical data which are just as real and need to be integrated into *our* view of "Israel's" future as the rejection of the gospel by the Jews and the beginning of the Gentile mission were facts which Paul had to acknowledge and integrate into his understanding of the role of Israel in God's ongoing redemptive history. Nevertheless, it is difficult to see that Paul would have to change his basic answer were he alive today. It is doubtful that he would have to change his answer to the questions of when and how Israel will be saved. And to these we now turn.

The Future καιρός of Israel:
The Decisive Apocalyptic Hour

When will all Israel be saved? Romans 11:24 answers: "when the full number of the Gentiles comes in." The tradition of Mk 13:10 casts light upon the background of this answer: Before the parousia takes place the Gentile mission needs to be completed. When the gospel will have been preached to all nations, the parousia and also the salvation of all Israel will happen. The last phrase in 11:25 states the condition for the parousia and the simultaneous conversion of all Israel.

Bible translators and commentators are not agreed as to the exact significance of the word οὕτως at the beginning of v 26. Does it have temporal meaning and should we translate "*then* Israel will be saved?"[43] Or does οὕτως have a modal sense: "And this is *how* all Israel will be saved"?[44] In both cases, the begin-

---

42. So Michel, *Der Brief,* 358; Käsemann, *Romans,* 316; for νῦν as the original reading see the *Greek NT,* Nestle-Aland[26], and GNB.

43. NEB: "*When that has happened,* the whole of Israel will be saved"; Käsemann, *An die Römer,* 298: "sodann."

44. So GNB. The RSV gives a similar translation: "and so all Israel will be saved." The model meaning is preferred by Schlier, *Der Römerbrief,* 338; Michel, *Der Brief,* 355; Cranfield, *Romans,* 2:576; Wilckens, *Der Brief,* 2:255.

ning of v 26 is taken as referring back to v 25 and not forward to the Scripture quotation in vv 26b–27.[45] The meaning is in any case that "Israel will be saved as Paul has stated it in the immediately preceding sentences, namely, out of the midst of hardening and the already threatening consequences of rebellion (11:9–10), and only after the full admission of the Gentiles," which was a consequence of Israel's refusal to accept the gospel. In other words, Israel will be saved in a miraculous way.[46] The salvation of Israel will be part of the eschatological drama; it will take place at the end of history as we know it.

If Israel's salvation is viewed as a strictly eschatological event, 11:15 makes good sense: "For if their rejection means the reconciliation of the world, what will their acceptance mean but life from the dead?" Käsemann notes that "The phrase 'life from the dead,' which reminds us of the tradition in, e.g., Jn 5:24 . . . is not to be given in a transferred sense. It designated . . . what Paul elsewhere calls ἀνάστασις νεκρῶν and thus refers to the parousia."[47]

Schlier concurs with Käsemann: "It is presupposed that the final salvation of Israel is an eschatological event in the strict sense, an event which belongs to the general resurrection of the dead."[48] And Otto Michel specified: " 'Life from the dead' is not only an apocalyptic happening, which follows other processes, but most of all the final gift of salvation. There is no thought of a special 'spiritual awakening of Israel' or of a messianic fulfillment of the promise."[49] Michel's comments apply undoubtedly also to 11:26ff.

According to 11:26b–32 Israel will not obtain salvation through a "mass conversion" preceding the parousia, but uniquely and solely through an initiative of the God who has mercy upon all, an initiative totally independent of the attitude of Israel and of the rest of humanity.[50]

If this view of Israel's salvation at the end of days, at the time

45. The RSV reads a semicolon after "and so all Israel will be saved." The GNB reads a full stop.
46. So Wilckens, *Der Brief,* 2:255.
47. Käsemann, *Romans,* 307.
48. Schlier, *Der Römerbrief,* 379.
49. Michel, *Der Brief,* 346.
50. F. Mussner, "Ganz Israel wird gerettet werden' (Rm. 11,26)," *Kairos* 18 (1976): 250ff.

of the parousia, as a strictly miraculous happening through God's initiative, should be correct, *how* are we to conceive of it? How does it fit in with what Paul has to say elsewhere about salvation?

The Manner of Israel's Apocalyptic Salvation

The question concerning the time of Israel's salvation has been answered with its dating at the parousia. This already implies an answer to the question of the *how.* As we have said, for Paul, it will be a miraculous eschatological event. The apostle works here with an apocalyptic tradition that he drastically modifies. The core of the underlying tradition is "the apocalyptic expectation of the restitution of Israel and the associated pilgrimage of the nations to Zion."[51] J. Jeremias has collected the biblical evidence relating to this theme in his book, *Jesus' Promise to the Nations.*[52] The Old Testament and late Jewish tradition spoke of the eschatological glorification of Israel which would have a magnetic appeal for all Gentiles and would make the nations march to Zion (e.g., Isa 2:2–4; 55:5; 56:6–8; 60:4ff.; 66:17ff.; Jer 3:17; Ps 47:9; Zec 8:20–22).[53] The factual course of history, as Paul has witnessed it when he perceived the hardening of Israel and the spread of the gospel among the Gentiles, forces Paul to revise the Jewish expectation. In fact, he turns it around: History has shown that the hardening of Israel has made room for the conversion of the Gentiles; conversely now, Paul expects the completion of the salvation of the Gentiles to be followed by the redemption of Israel.

In this sense there is a special way for Israel, but it is not a second way of salvation especially for Israel. The salvation of all Israel is distinguished from that of the Gentiles, but the manner of salvation will nevertheless be the same, namely, it will be the victory of the free grace of God that will save Israel.[54] The

---

51. Käsemann, *Romans,* 312; so also Wilckens, *Der Römerbrief,* 2:254f with references in n. 1145.

52. J. Jeremias, *Jesus' Promise to the Nations* (London: SCM, 1967).

53. Examples from the interbiblical period are found in the Testaments of the Twelve Patriarchs, 1 Enoch, 2 Baruch, 4 Ezra, Psalms of Solomon, Tobit, Sibylline Oracles, et al.

54. Mussner, "Ganz Israel," 252f.

hope the apostle has for the unbelieving Israel remains tied to grace and faith. We must not read 11:26a ("all Israel will be saved") without 11:23: "And even the others, *if they do not persist in their unbelief,* will be grafted in; for God has the power to graft them in again." This sentence contains the whole dialectic of divine *and* human action: The *Jews* will believe, and *God* will graft them in again!

Israel will be saved by grace alone. The emphasis on God's initiative has been unmistakable throughout Romans 9–11 (e.g., 9:15–18, 25–26; 10:20; 11:8, 23, 31–32). What matters is not human will or exertion but God's mercy (9:16). "He has mercy upon whomever he wills" (9:18). He is free to create vessels of wrath or vessels of mercy (9:21–24). After God has shown his mercy to the Gentiles, he will show his mercy to all Israel (11:30–32).

The immediate context of the sentence "all Israel will be saved" (11:26a) underlines the same thought, namely, that the future redemption of all Israel will be by grace alone. Verses 26b and 27 are a comment upon the manner of Israel's restitution:

> The Deliverer will come from Zion,
> he will banish ungodliness from Jacob;
> and this will be my covenant with them,
> when I take away their sins.

For Paul, the deliverer who will come from Zion is the Christ of the parousia. The rabbis, too, interpreted Isa 59:20f. messianically.[55] The gift of salvation the deliverer brings consists in the forgiveness of sins (11:27b). Through the forgiveness of sins, Israel will be taken into the new covenant that Christ has established through the gift of his own life (Jer 31:33; 1 Cor 11:25 cf. Mk 14:24). The ground of salvation is the same for the church, consisting of converts from among the Jews and the Gentiles, and for the "rest" of Israel who are to be saved. God's redemptive action in the death and resurrection of Jesus Christ is and remains the sole foundation for the ultimate well-being of all humankind, including all Jews. The way or the manner of salvation is the same for all, only the time of their salvation differs. The rest of Israel will be saved by grace alone but not until the clock strikes "12" midnight.

Israel will be saved by faith alone. The emphasis on "faith apart from works" is equally unmistakable throughout Romans

55. Michel, *Der Brief,* 356 n. 10.

9–11. The "rest" of Israel is hardened not because they are morally wicked, but rather because they strive for works righteousness; they do not pursue righteousness through faith; they do not allow God to put them right in the way in which he wants to do so (9:30–33). Human faith remains crucial for obtaining God's salvation: "For man believes with his heart and so is justified, and he confesses with his lips and so is saved" (10:10). This applies to both Jew and Greek (10:12–13). Any person stands fast only through faith (10:20). But if the "rest" of Israel will "not persist in their unbelief," i.e., if they come to have faith, they will be grafted into the original olive tree (11:23). Conversely, the believers who do not continue in faith and in God's kindness will be cut off (11:17–22). (Paul never said, "Once saved, always saved.")

Considering the fact that Paul emphasizes both grace and faith in his treatment of the problem of Israel, we must conclude that Paul conceived of an apocalyptic, miraculous salvation of all Israel at the time of Christ's parousia in such a way that it does not contradict Paul's doctrine of justification and that Israel's collective redemption does not make superfluous the conversion of the individual Jew.

Today both Protestant and Catholic exegetes can be quoted in support of an interpretation that understands Romans 9–11 as holding together the expectation of a miraculous salvation of all Israel in the eschaton and the teaching of Paul that salvation is by grace through faith alone.[56] Perhaps, we can appreciate this difficult mode of thought on the part of Paul more easily when we remember that in biblical thinking divine and human action are not perceived as completely separate.

—God speaks *through* the word of the prophet

—Jesus said: "He who hears *you,* hears *me*."

—God is at work not only "above" us, but also "in" us and "through" us

—Paul can say: "work out your own salvation with fear and trembling; for God is at work in you, both to will and to work for his good pleasure" (Phil 2:12–13; cf. Eph 2:8–10: "For by grace you have been saved through faith; and this is

---

56. Käsemann, *Romans,* 310f.; Mussner, "Ganz Israel," 252f.

not your own doing, it is the gift of God—not because of works, lest any man should boast. For we are his workmanship, created in Christ Jesus for good works, which God prepared beforehand, that we should walk in them.")

—According to Rom 1:24, 26, 28, there is an intricate relationship between God's wrath and humanity's sin: God punishes the sinner by letting him sin more, by giving him up to the power of sin.

—The paradox of God's counsel and human responsibility is illustrated by Mt 26:24: "The Son of man goes as it is written of him, but woe to that man by whom the Son of man is betrayed!"

—For Paul, baptism is both a divine act of God and a human act. God acts by uniting us with Christ in his death and resurrection life, and we act by committing ourselves to Christ as our crucified and risen Lord. (The failure to grasp the dialectic of divine and human action lies at the root of our controversies about the Christian sacraments.)

Romans 9–11 is permeated with this thinking on both levels, the divine and the human, with correspondences on both levels. (I like to call it "double-decker thinking" for want of a better metaphor.) One will have noticed that in Phil 2:12–13 and Eph 2:8–10 the same mode of thinking is applied also to salvation, to God's and humanity's roles in it, to divine grace and human faith. Even the birth of faith in the human heart is a gift of God's grace. This agrees with the experience of the believer. We may think of

—Paul's experience on the Damascus Road, which was the result of God's revelation of his Son to Paul (Gal 1:12–17) and in which Christ laid claim upon this man (Phil 3:12). Paul understood his total work in the light of this experience: "By the grace of God I am what I am; and his grace toward me was not in vain. On the contrary, I worked harder than any of them, though it was not I, but the grace of God which is with me." (1 Cor 15:10).

—The miracles of Jesus which awakened faith among his followers.

—The self-manifestations of the Risen Lord after Easter through which faith was born in the hearts of Mary Magdalene, Peter, and other disciples.

It should be possible to envisage a self-revelation of Jesus Christ to Israel at the time of the parousia that will awaken a faith response among the Jews who until then resisted the gospel of their Redeemer.

Possible Consequences

If the expectation of Israel's salvation is clearly fixed upon an eschatological event at the time of Christ's parousia, there are two possible consequences: (1) The fulfillment of Israel's future is not an "innerworldly" matter, and it does not consist of a number of steps leading to its realization. The hope Paul cherishes for Israel is not a national-nationalistic blessing in terms of an earthly possession. What Paul expects for his kinsmen by race is nothing else than what is offered in the gospel of Jesus Christ: the forgiveness of sins, a covenant with individuals established by God's love.

One of the more recent British commentators writes as follows on 11:26b–27:

> This composite quotation, then, points unmistakably, by its relentless concentration on God's forgiveness and on Israel's need of it, to the true nature of the deliverance signified by σωθήσεται. It dashes Israel's self-centered hopes of establishing a claim upon God, of putting Him under an obligation by its merits, making it clear that the nation's final salvation will be a matter of the forgiveness of its sins by the sheer mercy of its God. It is also to be noted that there is here no trace of encouragement for any hopes entertained by Paul's contemporaries for the re-establishment of a national state in independence and political power, nor—incidentally—anything which could feasibly be interpreted as a scriptural endorsement of the modern nation-state Israel.[57]

I think this observation is correct. If one wonders whether after almost two thousand years Paul might see a place for a nation-state of Israel, the answer can only be (as far as I can see) that Paul would reject the idea as a matter of the σάρξ, not in the sense of "sinful flesh" but as a "diaphoron," something irrelevant, probably as something that is passé. The reason would be that since the gospel is being spread in all the world, "Zion" is everywhere (as Jn 4:21–24 puts it: what matters is neither Jerusalem nor Mount Gerizim, but worship in spirit and truth), or

57. Cranfield, *Romans,* 2:579.

better: "Zion" is the "throne of God" from whom believers all over the globe expect their redeemer to come (cf. 1 Thes 4:16–17; 1 Cor 15:51–57).

(2) There is the question of the legitimacy of a "mission among the Jews" in our times. Billy Graham once made the statement that in view of Romans 9–11 we should not undertake a mission among our Jewish contemporaries. F. Mussner agrees:

> If God himself has hardened the hearts of the Israelites, then, "logically," only he, and not the church, can lead them out of this hardening. Not the converted Gentiles save "all Israel'—an absolutely unbiblical thought—, but only God alone. The hardening and the salvation of Israel through God correspond with each other. The one who hardens is also the one who saves. The salvation of all Israel, which Paul announces in Rom. 11:26a, cannot be isolated from the thought of a preceding hardening caused by God himself . . . If all Israel will be saved by a special act of God, then the "mission to the Jews" is worthy of questioning. The "conversion" of individual Jews to the Christian faith must not be considered the "normal case," but rather as an exception, made possible, of course, only through God's grace.[58]

The argument seems plausible, but it is not finally convincing:

—it overlooks what we have said earlier, i.e., that God-Christ-Spirit become present in the preaching of the gospel and that God uses the church as his instruments.

—It also overlooks the fact that Paul himself did not draw such a conclusion. For him, the gospel is *now* the power of God unto salvation for both Gentiles and Jews (Rom 1:16f.; 2:17ff.) as surely as the whole mission of Jesus was one to Jews and Gentiles (Rom 15:8). According to Rom 10:1, Paul continued to pray for the salvation of the Jews, and he magnified his ministry "in order to make my fellow Jews jealous, and thus save some of them" (11:14, cf. 1 Cor 9:20).

Paul's Understanding of Salvation: The Ultimate Triumph of God

We do not want to conclude these comments on selected questions without calling attention to the fact that it was not by accident that the apostle devoted so much space to the question of Israel's future—and with this we come back to the ques-

---

58. Mussner, "Ganz Israel," 253.

tion of the understanding of the whole exposition of Romans 9–11. We block our approach to this text when we expect to find in it a dogmatic doctrine of predestination. This applies also to the sentence that represents the absolute climax of these three chapters, namely, 11:32, the concluding sentence before Paul breaks forth in a hymn of praise: "For God has consigned all men to disobedience, that he may have mercy upon all." The reader of Romans will recall another, but also analogous, sentence from a previous chapter. I am thinking of 5:18–19:

> Then as one man's trespass led to the condemnation for all men, so one man's act of righteousness leads to acquittal and life for all men. For as by one man's disobedience many were made sinners, so by one man's obedience many will be made righteous.

The thought of an ἀποκατάστασις is not present in either text, if by ἀποκατάστασις we mean the doctrine of the eventual and necessary salvation of each and every individual.[59] Rather, Paul is concerned with humanity's experience of lostness and salvation as such, with the old and the new Adam, the old world and the new creation—all of this as work and gift of God. Romans 11:32 proclaims "the fundamental divine law of all history."[60] Karl Barth saw in this verse the key and sum of the epistle, and C. K. Barrett found here the concentrated expression of the Pauline doctrine of justification in its deepest paradox.

As regards the function of the whole section (Romans 9–11), Käsemann has correctly observed that it "repeats the transition from 1:18–3:20 to 3:21."[61] Therefore, *these three chapters, expounding Paul's view of the future of Israel, of its miraculous apocalyptic salvation, throw additional light on the familiar maxim of humankind's justification by grace through faith.* They tell us how radically humanity is dependent upon God's grace and how careful we must be not to pervert human faith into another human work. No one will be justified by personal works or individual merits, no one. Even the most pious ones do not obtain salvation by their piety (11:20, 22). The saving God always acts as *creator ex nihilo,* and faith is always faith in

---

59. The latter is asserted by Kuss, *Der Römerbrief,* 3:929 but rightly contested by Käsemann, *Romans,* 316.
60. Käsemann, ibid.
61. Ibid., 317.

God who raises the dead—this is what Paul said of Abraham in
4:17 and of every Christian in 4:24; he says it explicitly of Jewish and Gentile Christians in 10:9–12, and in 11:15ff. he says the
same of Israel in the hour of her salvation at the time of Christ's
parousia. Furthermore, we learn that *"justification" is a personal but not an individualistic matter* "since God is . . . the
Creator of the world and not just the one who stands over
against individuals."[62] Therefore, Paul is not only concerned
about the individual converted or unconverted kinsman, he has
to be concerned about the people as a whole, indeed he has to
be concerned with the fate of all humankind. "Hence salvation
history in its universal breadth is linked to the doctrine of justification. It is not its superstructure but its horizon"[63] within
which Paul conceives of it.

> Paul is bold enough to view both each individual and world history
> from the standpoint of the doctrine of justification. The end of the
> world and the beginning of the new world can be thought of only
> as the justification of the ungodly.[64]

Thus the future of Israel must be seen from the same vantage
point.

62. Ibid.
63. Ibid.
64. Ibid.

THE SPIRIT IN 2 CORINTHIANS IN LIGHT OF THE "FELLOWSHIP OF THE HOLY SPIRIT" IN 2 CORINTHIANS 13:14

7

Ralph P. Martin
Professor of New Testament
Fuller Theological Seminary

NOT THE LEAST AMONG the valuable insights in George Beasley-Murray's commentary on 2 Corinthians is his brief notice of 13:11–14, and in particular of the Apostolic Benediction (v 14 [NA[26] = v 13]). He is one of the few commentators to raise the question of the function of v 14 in the setting of the situation Paul encountered at Corinth. He observes how "this was a church which was torn by factions, whose members had ranged themselves contentiously with different apostles . . . [and] at one point rejected Paul's authority, and through adherence to the heretical 'super-apostles' were in danger of rupturing relations with the rest of the churches in Christ." He concludes:

> If ever a church needed to learn afresh the meaning of *the fellowship of the Holy Spirit* it was this one—and not merely its meaning, but its reality.
>
> Accordingly, the benediction which Paul normally pronounced became expanded into a blessing of extraordinary pertinence to the church to which it was addressed.[1]

The purpose of this short essay, offered in tribute to George Beasley-Murray as a token of esteem and gratitude, is to explore in somewhat more detail than was permitted to him in a multi-volumed commentary the "extraordinary pertinence" of 13:14 to Paul's debate with his opponents at Corinth and his attempt to win back the church to the apostolic cause he represented.

---

1. G. R. Beasley-Murray, "2 Corinthians," *The Broadman Bible Commentary,* vol. 11 (Nashville: Broadman Press, 1971) 76.

The Form of the Benediction

This "verse of capital importance" (Allo[2]) is marked by several unusual features. In no other place does Paul bring together the three names of God, the Lord Jesus Christ, and the Holy Spirit (though his order is different). Moreover, the theological terms, "grace," "love," and "fellowship," are linked in a way that is without parallel in the Pauline corpus. Since our study is concerned with the last member of the godhead mentioned in the verse, the Holy Spirit, we may observe that, if a strict symmetry is adhered to, the troublesome genitive is explained. Clearly "the grace of the Lord Jesus Christ" and "the love of God" are examples of a subjective genitive; and it is, at first glance, appropriate that the third phrase should be so interpreted. So many commentators conclude: "The genitives should all be understood in the same way, i.e., as subjective: the prayer is . . . for the *fellowship* which the Holy Spirit creates to be a reality among them."[3] According to this view, the Holy Spirit is the author of κοινωνία ("fellowship"), and Paul's desire is that the Spirit may fashion a genuine unity among the believers by creating peace, harmony and, above all, a true reconciliation with one another and with himself as their apostle. The tenor of the preceding verses (11–13) is in keeping with this desire, endorsed by such paraenetic calls as "aim for restoration," "encourage one another," "be of the same mind," "live in peace," and "greet one another with a holy kiss." It is eminently fitting that Paul would want to round off this section of hortatory appeal with the prayer that the Holy Spirit may indeed produce the desired result of churchly harmony and amity: κοινωνία, which is his gift to be received and applied.

But this exegesis is open to some objection. First, κοινωνία, which has a wide range of meanings in Paul and, indeed, has several different nuances in 2 Corinthians (see 6:14; 8:4; 9:13), may well be rendered "participation in," thereby requiring an objective genitive to follow. This is a familiar Pauline usage in such places as 1 Cor 1:9; 10:16; Phil 3:10; and 2 Cor 8:4, where the context rules out any sense of the possessive genitive. Philip-

2. E. B. Allo, *Saint Paul: Seconde Epître aux Corinthiens,* Etudes bibliques (Paris: Gabalda, 1956) 343. But see the qualification in A. R. George, *Communion with God in the New Testament* (London: Epworth Press, 1953) 179.

3. Beasley-Murray, ibid.

pians 2:1 is problematic, but on balance, it is more likely that there the sense must be, in Paul's list of "grounds of appeal" on which he bases his call to the Philippians, "if there is any common sharing in the [Holy] Spirit" or "fellowship with the Spirit," as Seesemann renders the phrase τις κοινωνία πνεύματος.[4] Seesemann's main argument runs as follows: the apostle takes for granted the believers' possession of the Spirit as a fact of Christian experience (e.g., Gal 3:2). Then, there is the parallel with 1 Cor 1:9 just noted. The patristic testimony is next cited as in favor of the objective genitive. Finally, Seesemann establishes an argument based on the form of Paul's wording at Phil 2:1. The phrase in that verse, κοινωνία πνεύματος, is held to be joined to σπλάγχνα καὶ οἰκτιρμοί, "affection and sympathy." Together these parallel phrases denote what is internal to the Christian over against παράκλησις ("encouragement") and παραμυθία ("consolation"), which are regarded as outside the Christian's immediate experience, since they are objective standards to which Paul appeals. So the objective genitive is held to be the correct understanding, and Paul is appealing to the common life the church has "in the Spirit" as an "objective work" (to use Lohmeyer's designation[5]) in which they are called to share. This conclusion, reflected in the modern translations of the RSV, NEB, and NIV, but challenged by the most recent commentator on Philippians,[6] may be sustained. If it is a sound deduction, it raises at least the possibility that 2 Cor 13:14 is to be taken in the same way. This exegesis of Phil 2:1 overcomes an obstacle to interpreting 2 Cor 13:14 as containing a mixture of

---

4. H. Seesemann, *Der Begriff* KOINΩNIA *im Neuen Testament,* BZNTW 14, discussing the term *Geistesgemeinschaft,* "Spirit-fellowship," as though two ideas were fused into one (Geissen: Töpelmann, 1933) 72–73. J. Hainz, *Koinonia. Kirche als Gemeinschaft bei Paulus* BU 9 (Regensburg: F. Pustet, 1972) 48, dryly remarks that this rendering is more an illustration than an explanation. Seesemann's preferred exegesis is for *innage Anteilnahme am heiligen Geist* (ibid., 71, 73), i.e., "intimate participation in." See too M. McDermott, "The Biblical Doctrine of *koinonia,*" *BZ,* n.f. 19 (1975): 64–77, 219–33; P. T. O'Brien, "The Fellowship Theme in Philippians," *Reformed Theological Review* 37 (1978): 9–18; G. Panikulam, *Koinonia in the New Testament,* Analecta Biblica 85 (Rome: Pontifical Biblical Institute, 1979).

5. E. Lohmeyer, *Der Brief an die Philipper,* ed. W. Schmauch. KEK (Göttingen: Vandenhoeck & Ruprecht, 1956) 17.

6. G. F. Hawthorne, *Philippians,* WBC 43 (Waco, Tex.: Word, Inc., 1983) ad loc.

syntactical and formal characteristics. Both verses hold together different grammatical usages, and they do so in apparent contravention of what the readers may be led to expect, namely, a strict symmetrical pattern.

On form-analytical grounds, the breaking of symmetry that arises from taking the first two members of 2 Cor 13:14 as subjective, Christ's grace and God's love, and the κοινωνία τοῦ ἁγίου πνεύματος ("fellowship of the Holy Spirit") as objective, is defended and explained in a good argument offered by W. Kramer.[7] He proposes that the first two parts of the verse are a pre-Pauline formula taken over by the apostle. He has borrowed these phrases and enriched them by his own addition of the reference to the Holy Spirit. Thereby he has destroyed the congruence of a binitarian creed by supplying the idea that the Holy Spirit is not so much the giver of salvation himself as the gift in which all the members of the church share. The problem with this proposal and its appeal to a piece of tradition in v 14 is that it is unprovable.

C. K. Barrett[8] has remarked on the difficulty with the view of taking the genitive τοῦ ἁγίου πνεύματος as subjective, which he renders "fellowship given by," when we seek to link it with what follows. The connection with μετὰ πάντων ὑμῶν, "with you all," he says, is difficult, whereas if the objective genitive is the correct construction then it is a smoother transition from the earlier parts of the verse; and the climax is found in that Paul is wishing for his readers a "continuing and deepening" of their participation in the Holy Spirit. This line of reasoning, however, is by no means compelling, and it could just as easily be maintained that Paul is invoking the call to unity wrought by the Holy Spirit as a reality he wishes to see taking shape at Corinth.

So far we have observed that the ambiguous phrase with κοινωνία in relation to the Holy Spirit has a relevance to the letter—ending as expressing a wish-prayer[9] or a "wish for blessing"[10]

---

7. W. Kramer, *Christ, Lord, Son of God,* trans. B. Hardy, SBT 50 (London: SCM Press, 1966) 20b.

8. C. K. Barrett, *A Commentary on the Second Epistle to the Corinthians,* HNTC (London: A. & C. Black; New York: Harper and Row, 1973) 344.

9. G. P. Wiles, *Paul's Intercessory Prayers,* SNTSMS 24 (Cambridge: Cambridge University, 1974) 115.

10. R. Deichgräber, *Gotteshymnus und Christushymnus in der frü-*

by an appeal to Christian experience. Whether that appeal is grounded on a continued call to unity which the Spirit provides (as in Eph 4:3), or an exhortation to remember a common sharing in the Holy Spirit as the hallmark of being a Christian is a teasing *crux interpretum*. Recent study refuses to be compelled to a choice of either/or.[11] Paul may not have been as precise as we would wish him to be. And in any case, the two interpretations merge[12] once we are reminded that the "fellowship of the church" created by the Spirit (subjective genitive) comes about through "the common share in the Holy Spirit" (the objective sense) in which all believers participate. So the exegetical dilemma is largely an unreal one, and Paul's thought may well encompass both grammatical constructions.

The Invocation of the Spirit

We have yet to investigate the reason for the inclusion of the Holy Spirit in the closing appeal. Superficially it may be maintained that in a list of practical and paraenetic admonitions to unity in the Corinthian congregation it is fitting that Paul should close on the note of recall, expressed as a wish-prayer. In a verbless ending (13:14) he invokes the three persons of the Christian godhead to grant the request he deemed vital. The Corinthians should act in obedience to his message, referred to obliquely in 13:8 as "the truth," and in a return to his side. Here we see one more illustration of Paul's coupling of statement and injunction. Already God in Christ has acted in salvation history and by the Spirit has brought the church into existence.[13] Now the Corinthians are encouraged (in 13:11–14) to live out their calling and to respond to the Spirit's activity to fashion an authen-

ben Christenheit, SUNT 5 (Göttingen: Vandenhoeck & Ruprecht, 1967) 95.

11. See J. Hainz, *Koinonia* (as in n. 4) 61. Perhaps the time is ripe for a reconsideration of A. Deissmann's proposal that, since it is often unclear whether a Pauline genitive is objective or subjective, a third category needs to be considered. He calls this "the mystical genitive," or (better) "the genitive of fellowship." See his *Paul*, trans. R. M. Strachan (London: Hodder & Stoughton, 1926) 162–164. He is indebted to O. Schmitz, *Die Christus-Gemeinschaft des Paulus im Lichte seines Genitivgebrauchs* (Gütersloh: J. C. B. Mohr, 1924).

12. So E. Schweizer, *TDNT* 6:434.

13. J. Hainz, *Koinonia* (as in n. 4) 61.

tic κοινωνία in place of a disunity and discord that so marred their congregational life.

Or so it would seem. Closer inspection of the earlier sections of 2 Corinthians that touch on the role of the Holy Spirit shows that the solution to the Corinthian malaise was not so simple, and the threatened danger to Paul's gospel and his apostolate at Corinth was much more ominous. We may review the salient passages not in order of appearance in our canonical text, but in a way that seeks to connect the teaching into a pattern.

2 Cor 1:21, 22

In a section where Paul is defending his apostolic ministry against a charge of vacillation and consequent unreliability, he finds it needful to set his arguments on a strong theological base upheld by several stanchions. His own fidelity to his calling and work is championed in a context of the divine covenant faithfulness. Against the allegation that he acted as a person dominated by worldly impulse (κατὰ σάρκα, 1:17), Paul retorts that he has worked always with a true conscience and sincere motive (1:12). But that subjective appeal is not all; neither is it enough to answer his critics at Corinth. He must also invoke the legitimacy of the apostolic ministry in which he has a share. So he writes:

> Now it is God who confirms both me and you in our relationship to Christ. He has anointed us, set his seal upon us, and imparted the Spirit to us as a pledge [ἀρραβών] (2 Cor 1:22).

The center of this confession of faith which is also an *apologia* for the apostolic service he claimed is the biblical idea of "confirm," i.e., to validate an agreement or an arrangement into which one has entered by a promise. The Pauline verb βεβαιόω, which echoes its Old Testament counterpart, the root >-*m-n*,[14] has this sense, but it is also seen in the word-play Χριστός . . . χρίσας, "anointed . . . Christ" (2 Cor 1:21) with associated ideas of setting apart and commissioning as in "sealing" and in the description of the Spirit as a "pledge" (ἀρραβών). The "seal" is introduced presumably to endorse the notion of the

---

14. See W. C. van Unnik, "Reisepläne und Amen-Sagen. Zusammenhang und Gedankenfolge in 2. Korinther 1:15–24" in *Studia Paulina* in honorem J. de Zwaan, ed. J. N. Sevenster and W. C. van Unnik (Haarlem: Bohn) 215–34.

claiming of human lives as God's possession which is his rightful due, and "the Spirit" (τοῦ πνεύματος) may be understood not as a partitive genitive (as though there were two actions of sealing and giving the Spirit) but in the explanatory sense: "the seal, which is the gift of the Spirit." In other words, we suggest that there are three images here, not four:[15] God, Paul avers, has put both apostles and people into a relationship with himself by the actions which the three divine persons are involved. It is God who has guaranteed our salvation by his promise in the gospel; Christ, "the anointed one," bids us share in his messianic blessedness; the Spirit is imparted as a divine seal upon our hearts, which is the pledge of final salvation. This snatch of soteriological catechism is introduced in a defensive way to offer a plea for the apostolic ministry; and the piling up of ideas and images—with a notable use of participles in vv 21, 22, which is a telltale sign of quoted liturgical/baptismal material—is intended to repel the innuendo that Paul's ministry is not to be trusted because he has a flawed character and that there is no validity to his apostolic claims. His retort is to establish his claim on the basis of the data of Christian life and experience, which in turn is traced back to the gospel he was commissioned to proclaim (1:19). Not least among the items he lists as part of a common Christian inheritance is the Spirit's seal. The "seal of the Spirit" is put on God's people as a token of eschatological salvation which has begun but is not yet fully accomplished.[16]

2 Cor 5:5

Here in a different context the same emphasis on the "eschatological proviso" of "not yet" may be heard. In the middle of an elaborate disquisition of the resurrection hope Paul interjects the prospect, still obviously set in the future, of "being clothed" in a new, heavenly body (5:1, 2) so that "what is mortal may be swallowed up by life" (5:4). He continues: "The one

---

15. As Barrett, *The Second Epistle to the Corinthians,* 80, 81 states.

16. This issue is paramount in Paul's debate with the Corinthians as reflected in 1 Corinthians. See D. J. Doughty, "The Presence and Future of Salvation in Corinth," *ZNW* (1975): 61–90; A. C. Thiselton, "Realized Eschatology at Corinth," *NTS* 24 (1977–78): 510–26. The ἀρραβών of 1:22; 5:5 is a parallel term with ἀπαρχή in 1 Cor 15:20 (cf. R. P. Martin, *The Spirit and the Congregation: Studies in 1 Corinthians 12–15* [Grand Rapids: Eerdmans, 1984] 110).

who prepared us for this very purpose (is) God, who also gave us the Spirit as a pledge [ἀρραβών].''

It is not easy to see the logical flow of this sentence, and part of the meaning turns on how the participle κατεργασάμενος is understood, whether as "prepared" (so RSV) or "designed," "created," "shaped" (NEB) or in the plain sense of "made" (so Moule[17]). More difficult still to identify is the object of God's intention in Paul's mind expressed in the words εἰς αὐτὸ τοῦτο, "for this very purpose." C. F. D. Moule interprets that design as one of the process of exchange, not addition. "In requiring us to part with our present clothes [our bodily existence in this age], he has, nevertheless, given us a guarantee of something better to reassure us—the presence of the Holy Spirit.'' But this conclusion has been exposed to some questioning, not least on the ground that it marks a distinct shift and development from Paul's earlier teaching in 1 Cor 15:51–57 where the new body is added to and superimposed on the old, whereas in 2 Cor 5 Paul's expectation is that the new bodily existence will be known only as it is exchanged for the old. Paul's use of the double compound verb ἐπενδύεσθαι in 5:2, 4 may be a problem for this interpretation. But Moule appears to dispose of it by insisting that Paul's desire to receive the additional body as an extra coat without divesting himself of what is underneath is a hope that is not attainable since this is not God's plan for us. He has made us not to add on an extra but to be rid of the old at death,[18] and then to receive the new σῶμα πνευματικόν (cf. 1 Cor 15:44) in the resurrection. This sounds perilously close to affirming that God has made us for the purpose of dying, which, of course, is a conclusion Moule does not explicitly draw. What, in our view, is the important contribution to which this discussion has drawn attention is that Paul's eschatological expectation does seem to have changed in the space of time between his composing the two canonical Corinthian letters, and the prospect, however abhorrent of an interim, a *Zwischenzustand,* between the events of death and the parousia seems to have been introduced to meet a real need that arose in Paul's debate with the Corinthian opponents subsequent to 1 Corinthians.

17. C. F. D. Moule, "St. Paul and Dualism: The Pauline Conception of Resurrection" reprinted in *Essays in New Testament Interpretation* (Cambridge: Cambridge University, 1982) 200–221 (215 n. 30).
18. Moule, ibid.

In 1 Corinthians the nub of the argument is found in the different ideas of the time-line between the present and the future.[19] The errorists, as Paul judged them (1 Cor 15:12), evidently took a belief in baptismal resurrection very seriously. In a manner akin to the teaching in 2 Tim 2:17, 18, they affirmed that their "death" in baptism was the important turning point which ushered them into a new existence now, because of which there was no need to entertain any future expectation. The future hope of a resurrection in a new bodily existence was—for them—collapsed into a spiritual ecstasy to be enjoyed in the present. This was their reinterpretation of Paul's eschatology which he needed to redefine on the principle that "death" is still the last enemy (1 Cor 15:26) to be encountered as a prelude to resurrection.

But this background scarcely does justice to the subtlety of his treatment in 2 Corinthians chs 4, 5, and we are led to postulate a deviant emphasis of a more nuanced kind. What is at stake are the two forms of Christian existence ascribed to being "in Christ." The opponents now pressed their earlier (i.e., according to the data in 1 Cor) contention of a "realized" eschatology to the extreme of stating that the soul may attain to God here and now since it is already liberated from its prisonhouse of the body and set free to soar in mystical freedom to the divine. This teaching is in Paul's sights in 2 Cor 4:16–18 with its contrast of the "outer" and "inner" person, and the heart of the present debate is seen in 5:7: "for we live by faith, not by sight." The last term, διὰ εἴδους, is the key;[20] it has a clear reference point in what is "seen," i.e., in the evidential tokens of visionary or ecstatic experiences in which sense perception played a significant role. Paul denies this access to reality in 4:18 because of his doctrine of "faith," and will return to the problem under debate in 12:1–2. For him the human person is treated as a unified whole, not to be dichotomized into "soul" (meant to be saved and united with the divine) and "body" (destined to be discarded as immaterial and inimical to the

---

19. I may refer to *The Spirit and the Congregation* ch 7 for some discussion.

20. As R. Bultmann, *The Second Letter to the Corinthians,* trans. R. A. Harrisville (Minneapolis: Augsburg, 1985) 141, 142 shows.

soul's highest interests[21]). In v 6, which continues the theme of 5:1–5, the phrase "in the body" (ἐν τῷ σώματι) is central, and this present bodily existence is for Paul all-important, since (a) present redemption affects our existence here and now (1 Cor 6:12–20); (b) how Christians live "in the body" in this age is the basis on which they must expect to be judged at the final day (2 Cor 5:10); and (c) by linking 1 Cor 6:12–20 with 2 Cor 5:5 we see the connection between the indwelling of the Holy Spirit in the Christian's σῶμα and the prospect of a new, future bodily existence at the resurrection. Inasmuch as the Corinthian faction had imbibed the gnosticizing teaching that stressed a spiritual existence as the complete possession of the pneumatic Christian here and now, thereby excluding any future hope or present moral accountability, the role of the Spirit as a pledge of what is to come was being effectively denied. Paul's allusion to the interim between death and the parousia may, therefore, have a polemic cast and be part of his larger concern to establish the element of "not yet" in his teaching of a bodily existence that is ours now in hope of a new bodily existence then, with the Holy Spirit as the bridge connecting the two. The Spirit conjoins promise and fulfillment.

2 Cor 3:1–18

The part given to the Holy Spirit in Paul's obviously self-defensive posture throughout this section is noteworthy. Aside from the use of a phrase, "the Spirit of the living God" (3:3), which is unique in biblical literature, the chief focus of attention is on the axiom of 3:6: "the letter kills, but the Spirit gives life," and on the idea of 3:17–18, which sums up the climactic effects, as Paul saw them, of "the ministry of the Spirit" over against "the ministry that leads to death, engraved in letters of stone" that belonged to Moses (3:7, 8).

The central theme of the chapter is διακονία,[22] "ministry." This term has to be read not only as part of Paul's midrashic ex-

---

21. Cf. F. T. Fallon, *2 Corinthians.* NT Message 11 (Dublin: Veritas, 1980) 47, 105.

22. See I. I. Friesen, *The Glory of the Ministry of Jesus Christ. Illustrated by a Study of 2 Cor 2:14–3:18.* Theologischer Dissertationen 7 (Basel: Fr. Reinhardt, 1971); and cf. R. Y.-K. Fung, "Justification by Faith in 1 & 2 Corinthians," in *Pauline Studies. Essays Presented to F. F. Bruce,* ed. D. A. Hagner and M. J. Harris (Grand Rapids: Eerdmans, 1980) 251–54.

position of the two covenants, Moses' and the new covenant of righteousness that is entrusted to the apostles. It has equally to be seen as in response to a more nuanced debate that Paul will have to engage in when the emissaries come on the scene at 11:4 and lay claim to being "Christ's servants" (διάκονοι) and "servants of righteousness" (11:15, 23).

It is a likely suggestion that Paul is driven here (in ch 3) to give a more sharply focused view of his Jewish-Christian opponents' teaching since his apostolic ministry is under fire.[23] The stark antithesis given in 3:6: "the letter kills, but the Spirit gives life," is capable of several esoteric interpretations. Our preference, while not denying the way it may be held to illumine the following verses, is to take Jervell's simple solution.[24] He takes γράμμα to refer primarily to the "letters of recommendation" (3:1-3) brought on to the scene by Jewish-Christian preachers. By contrast, since Paul has no claim to human authorization (see 1:1: "apostle . . . by the will of God") and in any case has no letters to accredit him save in the sense of 1 Cor 9:1, he appeals to his ministry as authenticated by the power of the Spirit who gives life from the dead (2:16). The issue behind the antithesis is exactly the question of rival ministries. It centers on the matter of who has the "principle of legitimation" (*Legitimitätsprinzip,* in Käsemann's term[25]) to support him, as in 13:1-4. In a nutshell, the opponents stressed their continuity with the past (the OT, Moses) and their present status. Against this *Traditionsprinzip* Paul emphasized discontinuity with the past, since the new age of the Spirit had come and the Spirit is the "pledge" (ἀρραβών) of the future which is open.[26]

The rhetorical question (in 2:16): "and who is adequate for this [kind of ministry]?" probably contains more than a hint that Paul is replying to the criticism that he was not competent (ἱκανός) to exercise any legitimate ministry at Corinth—a point against him

23. D. Georgi, *Die Gegner des Paulus im 2 Korintherbrief,* WMANT 11 (Neukirchen-Vluyn: Neukirchener Verlag, 1964) 241-73.

24. J. Jervell, *Imago Dei. Gen 1, 26f. in Spätjudentum, in der Gnosis und in den paulinischen Briefen,* FRLANT 76 (Göttingen: Vandenhoeck & Ruprecht, 1960) 178-79.

25. E. Käsemann, *Die Legitimität des Apostels. Eine Untersuchung zu II Korinther 10-13* (Darmstadt: Wissenschaftliche Buchgesellschaft, 1956) 34.

26. J. H. Schütz, *Paul and the Anatomy of Apostolic Authority,* SNTSMS 26 (Cambridge: Cambridge University, 1975) 175-76.

to which he will return at 10:12–18.[27] His answer is sought in the claim that it is "the ministry of the Spirit" he is commissioned (as in 1:19–22) to fulfill. Against the backdrop of a rival ministry, represented by the Jewish-Christian preachers (2:17) who took their stand on the example of Moses, a larger-than-life figure as interpreted by hellenistic Judaism, Paul expounds the validity of his apostolic role as a "minister of the new covenant," presumably being led to this rare phrase from his allusion to Jeremiah 31 in 3:3. The Spirit, however, is the link term connecting Paul's gospel of divine righteousness to his exercise of διακονία. Moses' limitations are stated in several facets, based on Ex 34:29–35, namely, (a) that the radiance (δόξα) on Moses' face was too awesome to behold, whereas the age of the Spirit is invested with a glory that gives "eternal" (i.e., belonging to the new aeon) life (3:6). The verb "to give life" is rightly regarded by G. Barth[28] as a polemical term, and constitutes the criterion and norm for understanding the apostolic preaching office (2:16: "an aroma of life"); (b) the glory that did invest the old order had its limitations, chiefly in that it led to "condemnation" (3:9), where the new aeon of the Spirit brings with it the gift of divine "righteousness" (v 9); and (c) the aura of splendor that illumined Moses' face lasted only briefly (v 13) in contrast to the radiance of the Spirit that is ever-increasing ἀπὸ δόξης εἰς δόξαν (v 18), "from degree of glory to another." This progression is directly attributable to the working of the Spirit who so reveals Christ that all Christians (v 18: (ἡμεῖς . . . πάντες) are enabled, with open face, to behold the glory of the Lord and so to be transformed into his likeness (vv 17, 18).[29] The meaning of the cryptic sentence ὁ δὲ κύριος τὸ πνεῦμά ἐστιν is a deep mystery since it seems to confound Christ and the Spirit, but only superficially so. Much hinges on how we take

27. E. Käsemann, *Die Legitimität,* 43–51.

28. G. Barth, "Die Eignung des Verkündigers in 2 Kor 2, 14–3, 6" in *Kirche. Festschrift für G. Bornkamm,* ed. D. Lührmann and G. Strecker (Tübingen: J. C. B. Mohr, 1980) 257–70 (267).

29. W. C. van Unnik, " 'With Unveiled Face.' An Exegesis of 2 Corinthians iii 12–18," *NovT* 6 (1963): 153–69. Some important correctives to this view, however, are supplied by W. H. Smith, Jr., "The Function of 2 Corinthians 3:7–4:6 in its Epistolary Context," unpublished dissertation, The Southern Baptist Theological Seminary, 1983.

the verb ἐστιν, "is,"[30] whether as the exegetical *significat,* "Now the Lord [in the passage Paul has just cited, Ex 34:34] *represents* the Spirit," or in a salvation-historical sense, with the meaning that the Spirit in Christian experience applies the saving acts of Christ and brings Christ within the reach of faith, so that his benefits may be received and shared. The same conundrum faces the interpreter at v 18 with the verbless phrase καθάπερ ἀπὸ κυρίου πνεύματος. The appositional words obviously go together, and we are pressed to define their relationship.[31] How is the Lord to be equated with the Spirit? Probably Paul is saying no more than that the Lord in the Christian saving confession (1 Cor 12:3) is the one whom we know as the Spirit in the sense to be nuanced in 5:16: though we have known Christ *qua* messiah of Israel from a human viewpoint (κατὰ σάρκα), now—in the new age of the Spirit—we have come to appreciate him κατὰ πνεῦμα, as exalted Lord (Rom 1:3, 4) by sharing in his Spirit (Rom 8:9). Once more participation in the Holy Spirit is the all-determinative factor which makes Christian experience authentic because it bears the hallmark of the new age—the καινὴ κτίσις of 2 Cor 5:17[32]—of which Paul's ministry speaks and by which it is legitimated.

Summary

The *norma normans* according to which Paul's apostolate is tested is, we may conclude from the point of view of this study, a sharing in the Spirit of Jesus Christ. That Spirit is the trait Paul invokes in 2 Cor 6:6, as later by extension he praises Titus for being a faithful exponent and representative of all that he stood for (12:18: "did we not walk in the same spirit and follow the same course?"). The spirit (πνεῦμα) is that of "faith" (4:13).

30. J. D. G. Dunn, "2 Corinthians III.17—'The Lord is the Spirit,'" *JTS* n.s. 21 (1970): 309–20; C. F. D. Moule, "II Cor iii. 18b etc." reprinted in *Essays in New Testament Interpretation,* 227–34.

31. We may cite Moule (as in preceding note, 232–34) for the unusual view that κύριος here refers to God (=Yahweh), not the exalted Christ. He takes κύριος to mean "the Lord (of the Exodus story) is (now, for us, represented by) the Spirit . . . as (is natural when the glory is) from a Lord (who is now experienced as) Spirit." We have preferred to retain the link of πνεῦμα with the heavenly Christ in the light of 1 Cor 15:45 and, more particularly, 2 Cor 5:16.

32. See P. Stuhlmacher, "Erwägungen zum ontologischen Charakter der καινὴ κτίσις bei Paulus," *Evangelische Theologie* 27 (1967): 1–35.

The easy transition from sharing in the Holy Spirit as a formula of life in the new age, begun but not yet finalized, to what is expected of those who live in that new world (2 Cor 5:17) paves the way for us to consider one remaining verse. In a key verse in the entire epistle (11:4) the emissaries whose preaching and living receive the severest condemnation as the work of Satan and as destined for perdition (11:13–15) are said to have introduced "an alien spirit" (πνεῦμα ἕτερον):

> For if the person who has come (to you) proclaims a rival Jesus, whom we did not proclaim, or if you welcome a different Spirit, which you did not welcome (in our message), or if you accept a different gospel, which you did not accept (as our gospel), then, you put up with this person right well!

There are many exegetical problems clustered in this single verse. The triadic structure with "Jesus," "Spirit," and "gospel" has been noted, and it is possible—but not likely—that πνεῦμα here means a counterfeit spirit replacing the Holy Spirit that Paul expected his people to have received at conversion and baptism (see Gal 3:2, with the identical verb λαμβάνειν; cf. Acts 19:2). More probably Paul's allusion is to the spirit of a lifestyle based on character which, in the case of their missionaries, so sadly belied their profession to be numbered with "the servants of righteousness" (11:15). On the contrary, their lordly bearing, selfish attitudes, and domineering outlook (11:20) leading to an encouragement of immoral ways (12:20, 21) are all sufficient evidence of their being "bogus apostles, workers of deceit, masquerading as Christ's apostles . . . [and falsely claiming a reputation] as servants of righteousness." The spirit they both exemplify by their wrongheaded ideas of apostleship and inculcate on the Corinthians is, for Paul, a betrayal of the gospel and apostleship, as he understood them. He therefore reserves only a "sentence of holy law" (11:15: "their fate will be what their deeds deserve") to express his abhorrence.[33] Their pretensions to charismatic power and their trust in ecstasy and signs (12:1–13) to validate their ministry were for him a complete denial of his "theology of the cross" and of the motif of strength-in-weakness which he had learned from the humiliated and lowly Lord (8:9; 12:10; 13:1–4, see 5–8; 4:7–12 for the relevance of

---

33. W. Baird, "Visions, Revelation, and Ministry," *JBL* 104 (1985): 661.

this model for Paul's ministry).[34] They do not share in that understanding of the kerygma which Paul first brought to Corinth (1 Cor 1:18–2:4). The tragedy is that the gullible Corinthians who ought to have recognized what a share in the Spirit means—from examples of Paul and Titus (see 7:5–16)—have turned away to this rival apostolate to embrace an alien gospel and to give hospitality to an antithetical spirit (πνεῦμα ἕτερον). See 11:19–21, which links with 11:4 by the hook-word ἀνέχεσθε "you put up with" these intruders and their teaching.

Conclusion

Each of the foregoing exegetical soundings has yielded a remarkably consistent result regarding the Spirit in 2 Corinthians, even if the precise settings are varied. Whether the topic is Paul's claim to valid ministry, or his insertion of the "eschatological not-yet" to oppose false dichotomy of soul and body, or the activity of the Spirit as actualizing the power of the new age in Christ, or the opposition to an alien gospel introduced with the blameworthy character of its proponents, Paul invokes the Holy Spirit with one master concern. He is seeking to establish the Holy Spirit as *the authentic sign of the new age, already begun but not yet realized in its fullness,* and he is building his case on *the readers' participation in the Spirit as the hallmark of their share in both the new world of God's righteousness and the Pauline apostolate that represents it.*

If this conclusion is near the mark, our revisit to 2 Cor 13:14 will alert us to the claim that the genitival phrase κοινωνία τοῦ ἁγίου πνεύματος should be preferably understood as objective. But that is not the really important item. Both our sharing in the Spirit and our preserving the ecclesial unity he creates are equally a Christian privilege and a Christian concern. What Paul is seeking to reinforce in this concluding wish-prayer is the assurance that it is the Holy Spirit who is at work. It is the Spirit of the *gracious* Lord Jesus Christ whose power is expressed in the *divine love* of his incarnate (2 Cor 5:14) and atoning (5:16–21) ministry that is available to his readers to make real Paul's call to reconciliation and renewal that has sounded throughout

34. D. A. Black, *Paul, Apostle of Weakness. Astheneia and its Cognates in the Pauline Literature* (New York: Lang, 1984) for a full exposition of this theme.

the different pieces of the letter(s) we know as 2 Corinthians. Hence it is altogether fitting that the final blessing-wish should run:

> The grace of the Lord Jesus Christ, and the love of God, and fellowship of the Holy Spirit be with you all.[35]

35. The translations of 2 Cor given above are drawn from the present writer's edition of *2 Corinthians.* WBC 40 (Waco, Tex.: Word, Inc., 1986).

JESUS AS LORD: THE DEVELOPMENT OF THE CONCEPT

8

I. H. Marshall
Professor of New Testament Exegesis
University of Aberdeen

IN THE PREACHING AND TEACHING of the early church the concept expressed by Jesus' use of the phrase "the kingdom of God" was given fresh expression in a variety of ways, and one of them was the proclamation of Jesus himself as Messiah and Lord.[1] The kingdom was in effect replaced by the king. The christological title most used to express this motif was that of Lord, and in this essay I want to explore the development and usage of this title for Jesus in the early church.[2]

There can be no doubt regarding the central importance of this concept. When Paul wanted to describe what made a person a Christian in Rom 10:9 he said, "If you confess with your lips that Jesus is Lord and believe in your heart that God raised him from the dead, you will be saved." This verse shows that the decisive mark of being a Christian was public confession of Jesus as Lord, and it is generally agreed that this confession was bound up with baptism. The evidence suggests that a person

---

1. I. H. Marshall, "Preaching the Kingdom of God," *ExpTim* 89 (1977-78): 13-16. On the whole topic see now G. R. Beasley-Murray, *Jesus and the Kingdom of God* (Grand Rapids: Eerdmans, 1986).

2. For bibliography, see H. Bietenhard, "Lord, Master," in C. Brown, ed., *The New International Dictionary of New Testament Theology,* 3 vols. (Exeter: Paternoster Press, 1976) 2:519f., with *Addenda* (1982), 10.

publicly expressed acceptance of Jesus as Lord at baptism. Obviously the outward confession was not enough, and two further factors entered into the picture. The first was that coupled with the outward confession with the mouth was the inward act of faith. Alongside confession of Jesus as Lord there is the faith that he really is the Lord, a fact that, as we shall see, is related to his resurrection. The second factor comes from 1 Cor 12:3 where Paul tells us that nobody can say that Jesus is Lord apart from the Holy Spirit. In other words, only the action of the Spirit can persuade us that Jesus is Lord and enable us to make our confession meaningfully. This is not surprising because faith and the Holy Spirit are like two sides of the same coin. What God does in us by his Spirit corresponds to what we do by faith. The important point is that the work of the Spirit at conversion is to lead us to confess that Jesus is Lord. Other Christian confessions existed, but this seems to have been the primitive one.

The Meaning of "Lord" in the Greek Language

What would this term "Lord" have signified to people who used it? If we confine ourselves to the Greek language in which the New Testament was written, the word κύριος could be used in a variety of contexts and ways:

(1) One of its most frequent uses is simply as a title of respect in addressing other people. In English we use "Sir" in this kind of way, sometimes simply as a mark of politeness to people whom we don't know or with whom we have only a rather formal relationship, at other times as a mark of respect for the dignity of somebody else. The word was clearly used in this way in Greek (Mt 27:63).

(2) In particular, it could be used in this way to address an older person or somebody of a higher social class. It appears to have been the word used by pupils to address a teacher, and it corresponded to the use of "teacher" or "rabbi" by the Jews (Mt 8:25 diff. Mk 4:38; Mt 17:15 diff. Mk 9:17).

(3) Next, it could be used to mean a master, the owner of property (Mk 12:9; Lk 19:33) or slaves (Lk 12:42f.; Eph 6:5) or even a husband in relation to his wife (1 Pet 3:6). Anybody who stood in a legal relationship of superiority or ownership was a

"lord" or "master" to the people beneath him.

(4) It could be used of political rulers, and in the first century it was particularly used of the Roman emperor (Acts 25:26) and expressed his absolute authority. It corresponded to the Latin term *dominus*. It did not in itself mean that the ruler was divine, but it could be used so closely with divine terms that it probably acquired something of the flavor of divinity.

(5) Finally, the term was used of the gods who have power and rights over humankind (1 Cor 8:5), and it could express a personal relationship to them. One particular usage was very important, and for this we now have to look at the Jewish background. In the Jewish Scriptures the name of God was expressed by the four Hebrew letters "YHWH" which were vocalized as "Yahweh." Over the years, however, the Jews became extremely reverential towards God and were frightened even to say his name aloud for fear of blasphemy. So they did not pronounce it, and in course of time the pronunciation was forgotten. There was another Hebrew word (*'ādōn*) which meant "lord" and was often used to describe God. Accordingly, when the Jews came to the name of God in Scripture, they substituted a form of this word for lord, *'ădōnāy*. When the Jewish Bible was translated into Greek, they replaced *'ădōnāy* with the corresponding Greek word for Lord, κύριος. They may not have done so with complete consistency in early days, but it seems probable that by New Testament times this was the word that was used.[3]

The Application of "Lord" to Jesus

Next we must summarize the ways in which the word Lord was used when it was applied to Jesus.

(1) The word was used as a polite form of address to Jesus, just as it was to other people. For example, the Samaritan woman in John 4 so addressed Jesus at a point in the conversation when he is still simply an unknown stranger (Jn 4:11).

(2) During his earthly life Jesus was addressed by various people as "Lord" or "Sir," often in the context of his being

---

3. J. A. Fitzmyer, "Der semitische Hintergrund des neutestamentlichen Kyriostitels," in G. Strecker, ed., *Jesus Christus in Historie und Theologie* (Tübingen: J. C. B. Mohr, 1975) 267–98.

known as a teacher. Sometimes he was addressed in Jewish fashion as "Teacher" (Mk 4:38) or "Rabbi" (Mk 9:5), and this term is then rendered in another Gospel by the Greek word "Lord" (Mt 8:25; 17:4). Mark has the Greek word only once, and it is used by the Greek-speaking Syro-Phoenician woman rather than by a Jew (Mk 7:28). It is Matthew and Luke who use it more frequently, and the question arises whether what was actually said was "Rabbi" (which was simply a title for a teacher) or rather the Aramaic word *mār,* which means Lord and was a more general term of respect for a lord or master.[4] But whichever word was used, it need not have been more than a term of respect for a teacher or a religious leader. However, sometimes the word is used by people who come to Jesus asking him to perform a mighty work, and such usage may include the thought of the authority that Jesus possessed and that enabled him to do such things.

(3) It is not likely that Jesus was thought of as a master of slaves, although in his parables he often has slaves addressing their masters with this term. In some of the parables the master may be a metaphorical picture for himself. One interesting point is when Jesus sends the disciples to get the animal on which he rode into Jerusalem; they are to say "The lord needs it" (Mk 11:3); it is not absolutely clear how the term is to be understood, especially when in the same story Luke tells how the disciples spoke to the animal's "masters," using the same Greek word.

(4) We saw that the word was used for political rulers. Jesus was not regarded as a political ruler, and indeed in his teaching he distanced himself and his disciples from the behavior of political rulers who sought power and glory. Nevertheless, the use of "lord" for political rulers is relevant to us because political rulers could demand loyalty, reverence, and even worship from their subjects, which in the eyes of Christians conflicted with the loyalty they felt to Jesus. Outside the New Testament we know that Christians refused to accept the dominion and divinity of the Roman emperor, and there can be little doubt that they saw opposition between calling Jesus Lord and calling the emperor Lord in any absolute sense. When Jesus is called "king of

---

4. See F. Hahn, *The Titles of Jesus in Christology* (Guildford: Lutterworth, 1969) 73–89; Ph. Vielhauer, *Aufsätze zum Neuen Testament* (Munich: Kaiser, 1965) 150–57.

kings and lord of lords" (Rev 17:14; 19:16), his supreme lordship is expressed. However, it does not seem likely that Christians called Jesus "Lord" in imitation of political rulers; rather,
it was because they regarded Jesus as their religious lord that
they began to define his lordship as superior to that of political
rulers.

(5) Finally in this survey of usage we have the use of "lord"
for objects of religious veneration. This could have happened
in two ways. On the one hand, Paul tells us that there were
many so-called gods and lords in the world of his time, but for
Christians there was one God, the Father, and one Lord, namely,
Jesus Christ (1 Cor 8:5f.). Here the rivalry between Jesus and
pagan gods is expressed, and it is evident that Jesus is thought
of as superior to pagan gods; indeed, in Paul's view they are not
gods and lords at all, that honor being reserved for the objects
of Christian worship. On the other hand, the title of "Lord"
ranged Jesus alongside God the Father. The New Testament
does not often call Jesus God directly, but it certainly takes over
the Old Testament use of κύριος to refer to God and reapplies
it to Jesus. Passages of Scripture that originally applied to God
are reapplied to Jesus, thereby showing a tacit identification of
Jesus with the Lord spoken of in the Old Testament. So much so
is this the case that it is true to say that the word "Lord" in a
religious sense is applied to Jesus more often than to God the
Father in the New Testament. It appears that the Christians
needed a new terminology to express the place of Jesus alongside God. They had two solutions. One was to speak of Jesus as
the Son alongside the Father; the other was to appropriate one
of the titles for God, namely Lord, for him and to reserve the
title of God for the Father, and by and large they kept to this use
of the titles.

The Functions of Jesus as Lord

Having surveyed briefly the ways in which the term Lord
could be applied to Jesus in relation to the existing uses of the
word, we must now ask what were the implications of the title
when it was applied to Jesus. What was it used to convey?

(1) When we look at the developed thought of the New Testament, it is clear that Jesus was regarded as Lord in relation to
the act of creation. First Corinthians 8:6 tells us that there is

one Lord through whom are all things and through whom we exist. Although some scholars take this to refer to the present lordship of Christ over creation—and that in itself is a staggering thought—I take it that the text refers to creation and contains the assertion that the preexistent Christ had a part in the work of creation.[5] It is the same thought as in Heb 1:2 where creation is associated with the status of Jesus as Son.

(2) It follows that at this stage in thinking Jesus is regarded as Lord over the whole of creation. There will come a point when all the powers in the universe will be finally subjected to him, even though at present they may still be in active rebellion. In Phil 2:9–11 Jesus is granted the name that is above every name; this is surely the name of Lord. By virtue of it everything in creation will bow before him and confess that he is Lord. The confession made by Christians here and now will one day be made by all creation, although it is not said that this will be the means of their salvation. The thought is of triumph rather than of redemption.

(3) In a more personal way Jesus is the Lord of those who believe in him. They confess him as Lord at their conversion and baptism. He is their Lord by virtue of the fact that he has redeemed them and bought them to be his own. Using a different Greek word, 2 Pet 2:1 criticizes those who deny the Lord (δεσπότης) who bought them. A sense of personal devotion emerges in Thomas's cry to Jesus, "My Lord and my God" (Jn 20:20) or when Paul speaks of the surpassing worth of knowing Christ Jesus "my Lord" (Phil 3:8). Adoring worship and communion characterize such phrases.

(4) As a result, Paul particularly can speak to Christians "in the Lord." This phrase has much the same force as "in Christ" and expresses that the life of the believer is determined by the fact of Christ, the crucified and risen Lord. Thus Paul can command his readers to do certain things "in the Lord" (Eph 6:1; Col 3:17; 2 Thes 3:12), and it is thus with the Lord's authority that he issues his commands to believers. Here is the outworking of their personal acceptance of Jesus as their Lord: they must do what he says.

(5) Finally, the hope of Christians is tied up with the coming

5. J. D. G. Dunn, *Christology in the Making* (London: SCM Press, 1980) 179–83.

of the Lord. They pray "Maranatha" ("Our Lord, come"[6]), and it is this hope that fills their horizon (1 Cor 16:22). The New Testament ends with the call to Jesus, "Come, Lord Jesus" (Rev 22:20), both as the object of personal devotion and as the Lord who will bring all war and opposition to an end.

The Development of the Belief that Jesus Is Lord

Our next question is concerned with the way in which the understanding of Jesus as Lord developed in the early church. What was it that led to this remarkable estimate of Jesus? How did a man who had been crucified come to be regarded within a few years as the Lord of all creation, on a level with God himself? We must investigate the way in which the church was led under the inspiration and guidance of the Spirit to this full acknowledgment of the status and nature of Jesus.

The Theory of W. Bousset

Bousset argued that it was in effect the influence of the Hellenistic world that led the Christians to see Jesus as the Lord. He postulated that increasingly they began to see Jesus in the light of the pagan cults from which some of them had been converted. The person who had originally been revered simply as a teacher and prophet was increasingly assimilated to the kind of figure worshiped in pagan cults and so began to be regarded as spiritually present with his worshippers and as a person worthy of worship. Thus the recognition of Jesus as Lord was a second stage in the development of Christology; this was preceded by a first stage in which Jesus was not regarded in so lofty a manner.[7]

This theory is implausible, and one of the main reasons why it is implausible is that it cannot account satisfactorily for another text from 1 Corinthians, the verse that records the early Christian cry, "Maranatha." This cry has been preserved in Aramaic, and it was evidently used in a Greek-speaking church in that language. Bousset was forced to argue that its use arose in

---

6. It is difficult to be certain whether the Aramaic phrases represented by "Maranatha" should be understood as a statement or as a prayer, but the point being made is not affected.

7. W. Bousset, *Kyrios Christos* (Nashville: Knox, 1970).

Antioch where the church was bilingual. But it is much more probable that it arose in a church that normally spoke Aramaic and where the decisive theological development took place in an Aramaic-speaking culture. Moreover, we can trace a probable background for it in the book of 1 Enoch, which is cited in Jude 14. Here Enoch prophesies that the Lord will come with his holy ones to execute judgment. No doubt the writer of Enoch was thinking of God as the Lord (cf. Zec 14:5). But early Christians applied the wording to Jesus, and prophesied and prayed that he would come in judgment. The point is that this text shows that Jesus was regarded as the coming Lord in the early Aramaic-speaking church, and this takes us back into an area influenced by Jewish ideas rather than Greek ideas. Consequently Bousset's view places the development too late and in the wrong cultural environment.[8]

The Theory of F. Hahn

The contemporary scholar F. Hahn has argued from the evidence of phrases like "Maranatha" that when the early church first used various titles for Jesus they were limited in reference to the future activity that it expected of him. That is to say, the church spoke of Jesus as Lord first of all in the context of his future coming, and it did so on the analogy of the future coming of the Son of man. Then, in Hahn's view, the church began to realize that if Jesus was to come as Lord, he was not merely the Lord-designate, but was already the Lord; he had been enthroned since his resurrection. Thus the church began to apply the title of Lord to the risen Jesus, and then eventually to the earthly life of Jesus.[9]

This view is part of a larger theory that is unsatisfactory at many points. The objection to it in the present context is that it does not explain how it was that the title of Lord came to be applied to Jesus as the future Coming One. It is easy to see the connection between the Son of man and the future coming of Jesus, since we have Daniel 7:13f. to give us the link. But why did the early church proceed from the future coming of Jesus to giving him the title of Lord? It is surely more probable that the

---

8. M. Black, "The Maranatha Invocation and Jude 14, 15 (1 Enoch 1:9)," in B. Lindars and S. S. Smalley, eds., *Christ and Spirit in the New Testament* (Cambridge: Cambridge University, 1973) 189–96.

9. F. Hahn, *Titles*, 89–103.

process was the other way round, namely, that the church began by believing that Jesus was Lord and then prophesied that the Lord would come. Thus we still have to explain why the church believed that Jesus was the Lord.

A Possible Solution

i. *The Teaching of Jesus* If we turn to the accounts of the earthly life of Jesus we may find some material to indicate what started this process. We have already seen that the disciples addressed Jesus as "Sir" or "Lord," but this in itself is hardly the starting-point for the process, since this phrase could be used to address any human being who occupied a position of superiority or honor. Even if Jesus said to his disciples, "You call me Teacher and Lord" (in words ascribed to him in Jn 13:13),[10] it is doubtful how much we are to read into the title. However, various other bits of evidence may be significant.

(1) In Mk 2:28 Jesus says that the Son of man is lord of the Sabbath. Here "lord" is not a title but more a description of a function. Nor is it used absolutely to mean "the lord" but relatively to refer to the lord of the Sabbath. Yet it is a tremendous assertion to make. What kind of man is it who can claim lordship over the Sabbath? Was not this the prerogative of God? Moreover, it is the Son of man of whom this is said. Here we have a link between Son of man and κύριος that could be significant.

However, it must be noted that there is some doubt whether this is actually a saying of Jesus. Even so conservative a writer as C. E. B. Cranfield thinks that this is a comment by the author of the Gospel about the significance of the incident and was not meant to be understood as a saying of Jesus.[11] Other scholars suggest that Jesus was making a statement that is true of humankind in general; they understand "Son of man" to mean "a man like me," "a man in my position," and not as an exclusive title.[12] Consequently, we must be cautious about our use of

10. Whether or not Jn 13:13 represents the *ipsissima vox* of Jesus, it accurately describes how his disciples spoke of him during his earthly lifetime.

11. C. E. B. Cranfield, *The Gospel According to St. Mark* (Cambridge: Cambridge University, 1959).

12. M. Casey, *Son of Man* (London: SPCK, 1979) 228f.; B. Lindars, *Jesus Son of Man* (London: SPCK, 1983) 102–6, regards the saying as composed by Mark on the pattern of Mk 2:10.

this verse, but it may well indicate that Jesus referred to lord-ship over the Sabbath in a way that was understood at an early stage in the church to signify his own position as Lord.

(2) In a number of parables Jesus refers to the absence of a householder who may come back unexpectedly and find his ser-vants either doing their duty as they should or else taking ad-vantage of his absence to misbehave. The disciples are to be like men waiting for their master to return (Lk 12:36, 37, 42, 43, 45, 46, 47; Mt 25:18, 19, 21, 23, 26). Here it is interesting that when Mk 13:35 has "You do not know when *the* master *of the house* is coming," Mt 24:42 has "you do not know on what day *your* master is coming." The point is that it would be very natural to transfer the name "master" out of its parabolic setting where it means the master of the slaves in a household to its application where it means the master of the disciples and specifically the Son of man who is to come in the future. We can see this trans-fer actually taking place in Matthew, and it could obviously have taken place long before the Gospel was written. Indeed it is implicit in Mark where the application of the parable is ex-pressed in parabolic rather than direct terms: "Watch therefore— for you do not know when the master of the house will come . . . lest he come suddenly and find you asleep. And what I say to you I say to all: Watch" (Mk 13:35–37). I see no reason to dis-pute the authenticity of this parabolic material and would argue that this use of "master" (though not necessarily the precise wording) can go back to Jesus.[13] Whether or not this claim can be sustained, it is obvious that, as soon as the early church rec-ognized Jesus as the coming Son of man, it would be natural for the term κύριος to be applied to him as the returning lord.

(3) Perhaps most significant is a brief dialogue in which Jesus asks the scribes how they can say that the Messiah is David's de-scendant, this being the popularly held view. Jesus saw an ob-jection. In a Psalm attributed to David, the author said, "The Lord said to my lord, 'Sit at my right hand till I put your ene-mies below your feet' " (Mk 12:35–37; Ps 110:1).

A word of explanation is necessary. The English and the Greek forms of the Psalm both use the same word ("lord" and κύριος respectively) to refer both the speaker and to the per-

---

13. The core of the parable at least goes back to Jesus: R. Pesch, *Das Markusevangelium* (Freiburg: Herder, 1977) 2:316f.

son addressed. However, in the Hebrew version the speaker ("the Lord") is "Yahweh" (for which *'ădōnāy.* would have been substituted in reading aloud) and the person addressed ("my lord") is *'ădōni* which means "my lord" or "my master." The confusion is avoided in printed English versions of the Old Testament which use "lord" both times but print the first occurrence in capital letters ("LORD") to indicate that the original had Yahweh. We might show the difference in spoken English by some such translation as "The Lord said to my master." There is no way of showing the difference in Greek unless one knows the context.

The point, then, is that the person addressed is called "my master" by David. Hence the problem for Jesus' hearers: on the assumption that a man does not normally regard his son or descendant as superior to him, how can the Messiah be David's descendant, if, as the Psalm says, he is superior to him? Jesus is making a novel point, namely, that the Messiah is David's lord. Furthermore, he asks how the traditional scribal understanding of the Messiah as a human descendant of David can be maintained in the light of it.

A simple way of understanding this question—or rather of answering it—would be to say that what Jesus is doing is to pose an insuperable obstacle to the scribes' view of the Messiah: the Messiah is not in fact a descendant of David, whether in the sense of literal descent or in the sense of being a person of Davidic character and rule. This solution is unlikely, however, since the early church firmly believed in the Davidic descent of Jesus, and this belief is found in early traditional material (Rom 1:3f.). The pericope as it stands, therefore, cannot have this sense, neither is it likely that it did so at an earlier stage in the history of the tradition; the early church's firm belief that Jesus was Messiah can hardly have arisen if it was known that he himself had firmly ruled out this possibility.

Second, if the question were inverted, the answer would again be easy. How can the Messiah be superior to David if he is his son? That question can be answered either by saying "The son of David is superior to David because God raised him from the dead and exalted him to be lord"—an answer that could only be given after Easter—or by saying "The son of David is superior to David because he is not only David's son but also the Son of man or the Son of God"; or one might combine the two answers.

Now if we go back to the original form of the question, perhaps the answer is essentially the same. We can paraphrase the question as, "How can the Messiah be, as the scribes say, [merely] a descendant of David, if as the Psalm says, he is superior to David?" And the answer is, He can still be what the scribes say he is, namely, the son of David by human descent, but it is more important to say that he is David's lord, inasmuch as he is also the Son of God/Son of man and/or he is specially exalted by God. It follows, incidentally, that if the Messiah is David's lord he is also the lord of people in general.

The significant points for our present purpose are: (a) Jesus here declares that the Messiah carries the title of "Lord"; (b) Jesus finds the evidence for this title in Psalm 110; (c) Jesus holds that what was said to David's Lord in Psalm 110 must be regarded as a prophecy to be fulfilled in the case of the Messiah.

Again the question of authenticity arises, and I would argue that the objections to this being a genuine saying of Jesus are unconvincing.[14] Yet even if this point is not granted, the pericope was probably in circulation at an early date.

From these three pieces of evidence we can now see that Jesus spoke in such a way about lordship that the question would probably arise for his disciples as they pondered on what he had said. If, however, the authenticity of these texts is questioned, they will still testify to a very early stage of thinking in the church.

ii. *The Significance of the Resurrection* The next step comes with the resurrection of Jesus. There can be no doubt that the emergence of the Christian church was due to the belief of the disciples that Jesus had risen from the dead and had appeared to them. How did they interpret this event? They saw it not only as the return of Jesus to life and not only as his raising up to heaven by the power of God, but also as his exaltation. A key text in interpreting what had happened was Ps 110:1, which they took as a prophecy of the exaltation of Jesus. The influence of this text is widespread in the New Testament. It is quoted in Acts 2:34 and Heb 1:13, and its influence lies behind the numerous places where Jesus is said to be at the right hand

14. I. H. Marshall, *The Gospel of Luke,* NIGTC (Exeter: Paternoster Press, 1978) 746f.

of God (Acts 2:33; 7:55f.; Rom 8:34; Eph 1:20; Col 3:1; Heb 1:3; 8:1; 10:12; 12:2; 1 Pet 3:22; Rev 5:1). It was cited by Jesus in Mk 12:35–37, the passage we have just discussed, and it also appears on his lips in Mk 14:62, where Jesus prophesies that the Son of man will sit on the right hand of Power and come with the clouds of heaven. The simplest explanation of all this is that Jesus himself spoke of the exaltation of the Son of man to the right hand of God, and that the early church then interpreted his saying as being fulfilled in his resurrection and continued to use the text which he had cited as expressing this belief. Therefore, once the resurrection had occurred, the recognition that Jesus was indeed Messiah and Lord was fairly automatic, and this is precisely what Peter asserts of Jesus in Acts 2:36. A parallel line of thought, starting from Jesus' claim to be the Son of God, led to the interpretation of Ps 2:7 as a prophecy of the begetting of the Messiah to new life (Acts 13:33).

But is this "simple" explanation defensible? The main difficulty is the unwillingness of many scholars to allow the authenticity of the various sayings attributed to Jesus, especially his use of Psalm 110 at his trial. But if this is not authentic, it is difficult to see what put the quotation in the minds of the early Christians and led them to interpret the resurrection as glorification and vindication.

iii. *Growth in Understanding in the Early Church* Once this step had been taken, the rest of the development can be traced. If Psalm 110 is seen to be fulfilled in the resurrection of Jesus, then this confirms that he is the Lord spoken of in the Psalm and the Messiah, and also that he is the exalted Son of man. Hence the dying Stephen speaks of seeing Jesus as the Son of man standing at the right hand of God. But it is the use of "Lord" which interests us, and here various strands of thought can be traced:

(a) There is a direct path to the earliest Christian confession. We recollect that the inward faith that accompanied the outward confession that Jesus is Lord was the belief that God had raised him from the dead (Rom 10:9). This confirms the evidence of Acts that it was the resurrection that was associated with recognition of Jesus' lordship.

(b) From this confession stems the personal relationship of the believer to Jesus as his Lord, which finds particular expression in Paul's use of the term "in the Lord" and in the general use of "the Lord" simply to mean "Jesus." Thus there also develops the use of the compound phrases, "the Lord Jesus" and "the Lord Jesus Christ," which encapsulate this confession and can become merely formal language if care is not taken. The title of Lord adds dignity to the name "Jesus" and to the compound "Jesus Christ."

(c) If Jesus is Lord after his resurrection, it is obvious that he must also have been Lord before it. The early church saw the resurrection as essentially the confirming of a status rather than the conferral of a new status. Admittedly some texts may suggest the latter. Thus Phil 2:9-11 suggests that the name of Lord was conferred on Jesus at his exaltation, and Acts 2:36 might be thought to point in the same direction. But alongside these we must put verses like 1 Cor 9:5 and 11:23, which see Jesus as lord in his earthly life. Hence it is not surprising that Luke can refer to Jesus as "the Lord" when describing what he said and did in his earthly life; this usage is in fact probably older than Luke. But it is significant that "Lord" as a formal title does not come into statements made by Jesus or his followers before his resurrection, in correspondence with the historical facts. One might compare how in John it is only after the resurrection that Jesus is spoken of as the Lord by his followers (Jn 20:2, 13; etc; cf. Lk 24:3, 34).

(d) If Jesus is Lord, it also follows that he will return as Lord. Hence we have the Maranatha cry. Jesus is not addressed or spoken of as Son of man, but the church uses the title that signifies his victory. But here another factor is becoming evident. We have noted the suggestion that Maranatha may reflect Jewish wording that originally spoke of God as the Lord who will come in judgment. This brings us to the fact that the early church saw Jesus as the Lord who was spoken of in various Old Testament texts where it was God who was originally meant. That is to say: sooner or later the title of "Lord," which originally referred to the exalted and victorious position of Jesus, was extended in meaning by applying to Jesus texts that originally spoke of God as the Lord. We can see this in the following examples: In 1 Thes 1:8 Paul refers to "the word of the Lord" (cf. 2 Thes 3:1; Acts 8:25; 12:24; 19:10, 20) by which he must mean the message about or from Jesus. This is an extremely common Old Testament phrase which refers to *God's* word to the prophets. In 1 Thes 4:6 Paul says that the Lord, namely Jesus, is an avenger, and he is probably alluding to Ps 94:1, which originally referred explicitly to the Lord as the God of vengeance. In 1 Thes 5:2 he speaks of the day of the Lord, another familiar Old Testament phrase that now means the day of the parousia of Jesus (see 1 Cor 1:8; 5:5; 2 Cor 1:14; Phil 1:6, 10; 2:16; 2 Thes 2:2; 2 Pet 3:10). In Phil 2:10f. Paul applies to Jesus the words of Isa 45:23, "To me every knee shall bow," which originally referred to God, the Lord, and it is interesting that in Rom 14:11 he uses the same text of judgment by God. In 1 Pet 2:3 Christians are said to have tasted that the Lord is good, an allusion to Ps 34:9 which originally applied to God. Christians are those who call on the name of the Lord (1 Cor 1:2, alluding to Joel 3:5).

What led to this process? Clearly it was facilitated by the ambiguity of κύριος in Greek, but in a passage like Psalm 110 anybody who knew the Old Testament knew the difference between "the Lord," namely, God, and "my Lord," namely, the Messiah. The same ease of transfer may have been linguistically possible in Aramaic if Lord was translated as *mār*, a word that was used both of God as lord and of human lords. But how did the Christians come to apply Yahweh-texts to Jesus? The process started fairly early, as 1 Thessalonians shows, although it is manifestly not the most primitive understanding of the title. Probably such phrases "the word of the Lord" and "the day of the Lord," which were simply Old Testament allusions and not explicit citations of specific texts, were the first to be used, and this led to the recognition that what was said of Yahweh in the Old Testament found some of its fulfillment in Jesus. Once the day of the Lord became the day of Jesus, the path was open to assert that the future functions of God would be carried out by Jesus. And of course this development was facilitated by the recognition that Jesus was the Son of God, the One who was the image and first-born of God.

All this development must have taken place quite early because we find that it is fully complete by the time Paul wrote 1 Thessalonians and Galatians. Thus he is able to say in Gal 1:1 that he did not receive his apostleship from man but through Jesus Christ and God the Father. Not only does he closely juxtapose Jesus and God, but he also contrasts them with men, thereby showing that for him Jesus is on the divine side of reality. Thus a number of factors will have contributed to the process whereby the functions of Yahweh were seen as fulfilled by

Jesus, and so Jesus was given an appropriate status.

(e) Does this then mean that the title of Lord when applied to Jesus in the New Testament eventually came to denote his divinity? To put the question in this form is inappropriate. The term "divine" is not used in the New Testament in any significant way. Further, Jesus is never identified *simpliciter* with God, since the early Christians were not likely to confuse Jesus with God the Father. Rather, they thought of Jesus as the Son of the Father, existing in his image, sharing his glory, and this means that they held that whatever was true of God in his nature and functions was also true of the Son, with the important qualification that ultimately the Son is subordinate to the Father. Now the title Son of God obviously expresses this point, at least in some of its uses. The question is whether the use of Lord carries the same implications. From our preceding survey it will be obvious that in many of its uses Lord does not have this deeper content. But when Jesus is called "the Lord" absolutely and when reference is made to his being given honor that puts him immediately below God the Father (Phil 2:11), then it is hard to resist the view that Jesus is being given a title which is tantamount to divinity as we understand it. But the number of places where this implication is present is limited.

Conclusion

The concept of Jesus as Lord brings out his sovereignty. He is king of kings and lord of lords. The title of king was rarely used for him (only in Acts 17:7; Rev 17:14; 19:16) and equally rare for God (1 Tim 1:27; 6:15). It meant "the emperor" in secular speech, as Acts 17:7 and 1 Pet 2:13 make plain. It is not clear whether this existing usage may have hindered its use. Because the kingship of Jesus was on a different plane from that of the emperor, there was no point in provoking trouble by suggesting rivalry. On the other hand, if "Lord" was a title used of the emperor, the same objections would surely have applied to using it. The term Messiah or Christ should have meant a ruler, God's agent in establishing a kingdom. But the term had this meaning only for Jews and could be taken to refer to a kingship that encompassed only the Jews or under which the Jews had superiority over the Gentiles. For whatever reason, the term lost the connotation of kingship and sovereignty, and it appears to have been understood more in the sense of redeemer or savior. The sense of kingship was preserved in the title of Lord, which would have been intelligible to all kinds of people. However, we should note that there could be a narrowing of meaning here, in that "Lord" tends to have a passive meaning; it signifies somebody who is to be obeyed and treated with honor, and it perhaps does not bring out sufficiently the active element of the exercise of kingship and dominion and indeed of granting salvation. Jesus is not merely the Lord to be obeyed; he is also the Savior, the Messiah who suffers, and therefore the full New Testament confession must be "Jesus *Christ* is the *Lord*," emphasizing that Jesus is both the Christ who saves us and the Lord whom we obey.

INDEXES

Author

Old Testament

New Testament